ends? Can we raise our value concepts to the truly universal status of a science and their use to the truly world effectiveness of a scientific technology? Or, as our present scientific and technological inventions draw human beings more tightly together into a complexly interrelated world community, must we continue to live, uncertainly, perhaps hopelessly, under the divisive sway of our prevailing value principles?''

Today's world is confronted with value problems of the greatest urgency. Since medieval times, our public life has been accompanied by colossal value conflicts and enormous human waste and wreckage, the author contends, and the ever increasing breakup of old ways of life in our rapidly shrinking world is magnifying incipient antagonisms, of which the Cold War is but one example.

"Something basically wrong has lurked in our culture, deep down in its institutional fabric, in its orientation and training, leading as if inexorably to mounting disaster. The question now is whether we can further afford this unenlightened and even illiterate mode of action, whether for bare survival, not to mention minimum or maximum gain, we dare remain, in our value considerations, in the unscientific semi-reflective ruts of the past. The belief behind this book is that this way of doing business is finished, or the great segment of the human race that calls itself civilized may itself be finished.''

D. W. GOTSHALK is a professor of philosophy and former chairman of that department at the University of Illinois. He also is a Fellow of the American Association for the Advancement of Science, a past chairman of the National Board of Officers of the American Philosophical Association, and a past-president of the American Society for Aesthetics. His other books include *Structure and Reality*, *Metaphysics in Modern Times*, *Art and the Social Order*, and *The Promise of Modern Life*.

PATTERNS OF GOOD AND EVIL

UNIVERSITY OF ILLINOIS PRESS, URBANA, 1963

PATTERNS OF
GOOD AND EVIL

A VALUE ANALYSIS • BY D. W. GOTSHALK

Other books by D. W. GOTSHALK

Structure and Reality
Metaphysics in Modern Times
Art and the Social Order
The Promise of Modern Life

To the Updegroves, Mary, Maida, and Mabel
with affection and gratitude

ACKNOWLEDGMENTS

I am indebted to the editor of *Ethics* for permission to use material from my articles "Outlines of a Relational Theory of Value" (1949) and "The Standard of Value" (1950), and to the editor of *Philosophy of Science* for similar permission in regard to my article "Value Science" (1952).

The Board of Trustees of the University of Illinois granted me a year of sabbatical leave to begin work on this book, and I wish to express my gratitude to the board and to the administrative officers of the university for this grant. I also owe thanks to the Research Board of our Graduate College for a subvention to finance preparation of the final typescript.

My debt to philosophers is far too extensive to be acknowledged in a brief statement. The footnotes are probably the easiest guide. To the best of my ability I have tried to take full advantage of the large amount of recent philosophical writing on value and value theory. My colleague B. J. Diggs has been most helpful in suggesting readings and my colleague M. H. Fisch in correcting the manuscript. Responsibility for the text, its coverage, phrasing, interpretations, and conclusions, however, is solely mine.

Urbana, 1963.

D.W.G.

PREFACE

Problems about values—good, evil, right, wrong, and the like—have existed as long as the human race. They have a certain sameness everywhere and always. Yet in each civilization and epoch they have certain differences, since human individuals and societies are diverse and in ceaseless change. In this book, I want to depict the general situation in which human values occur, analyze its components, and discuss its fundamental patterns. Then, I want to consider the extent to which it may be possible, in the light of this analysis, to solve what seems to me one of the fundamental problems about values in our own civilization.

This problem has been stated in various ways. A common but somewhat melodramatic way is to describe our current scientific and technological civilization, particularly its contentious, international politics and its smoothly rapacious commercial life, as immoral, in the sense of being based fundamentally on the belief that human beings and groups are means of personal or national self-interest, objects for use and loot, things to serve totalitarian, corporative, or otherwise organized aggrandizement. Ours is a power-hungry civilization, and what is needed before this wondrous product of science and technology destroys itself in its all-consuming passion for power, is to introduce into it some morality and human decency.

This provocative statement of the problem might be most acceptable, I think, if one of its assumptions were indubitable. This assumption is that we have on our shelves a ready-made and entirely adequate set of moral or value principles, and all that is needed is to insert them into our doings. Then, everything would right itself. This assumption, I believe, is mistaken. No such competent moral or value principles exist to perform this function. In truth, *they* are the problem. The basic difficulty is not with our technology and science, which generate our power, although these present difficulties. It is with our value concepts, the guides (among other things) of our science and technology. These concepts are divisive. Day in, day out, they divide human beings into contending agents and factions. Many of these concepts are archaic and prescientific, borrowed from the remote past, accepted on faith or by custom, and sustained by long-established dogmatic authority. Others, begun in philosophical reflection, have hardened into creeds as partisan and inflexible as prescientific beliefs, and are enforced with a similar dogmatism. Still others, most profound of all, shared by all factions equally but unconsciously, typified by an exaggerated individualism and a power-hungry creativity, have grown unreflectively into the basic fabric of the modern world, and form perhaps the most sturdy and primitive roots of its conflicts.[1] And the best value thinking, illustrated by the work of a few isolated philosophers, is supported by no suitable large-sized institutional framework, nor by any such framework at all, and languishes in a shadowy and vigorless twilight.

Our science and technology, I say, are not the problem. Indeed, the great need is to raise our moral principles and value concepts to the stature of our science and technology. Our scientific statements have universal validity. What is true in a science at one place is true of the same things at any other place, or its differences are explicable in a universally acceptable manner. Our technology has a parallel world-wide effectiveness. The pressing problem is to discover whether a similar universality and world effectiveness can be achieved in the value area, and can be institutionally as deeply implanted and as widely diffused in world culture. Can a

---

[1] D. W. Gotshalk, *The Promise of Modern Life* (Yellow Springs, Ohio: Antioch Press, 1958). Chapters I through IV describe these concepts in some detail.

balance be created between the two great halves of our civilization, our means and our ends? Can we raise our value concepts to the truly universal status of a science and their use to the truly world effectiveness of a scientific technology? Or, as our present scientific and technological inventions draw human beings more tightly together into a complexly interrelated world community, must we continue to live, uncertainly, perhaps hopelessly, under the divisive sway of our prevailing value principles?

Let me say at once that the topical question we are raising here is not at all whether a *natural* science of values is possible. A natural science of values, depicting what people actually prefer or value, the causal patterns of their preferences, what value choices result in what actions, the uniformities of value behavior, and more, is not only possible, but has been under construction for some time. To raise it as a problem would be several decades out of date, and certainly it would need no sustained argument, such as a book, to establish it as a live possibility. The basic problem of our civilization, to which we wish to direct attention, is rather this: are natural science and technology in all their forms including a natural science of values a very special case in the development of our culture, or do they represent a cognitive stature and a general level of achievement that can exist in equal degree but in a specifically different way in other and specifically different areas, and in particular in the value area in its unique aspect of providing proper guide lines to man's personal and interpersonal actions and his uses of natural energies?

While this question will be the main topical problem of this book, a good part of our time will be occupied with systematic problems of value. Their discussion is necessary, I think, before any satisfactory solution of our topical problem can be reached. To determine whether it is possible to bring our thinking about the proper guide lines of our conduct to the cognitive and technical stature of our natural science and technology, we must know first what value is, and what we *can* know about it. Specifically, what we must understand is the situation in which human values occur, the diverse components of this situation, the various ways the values in these components can be interpreted, and how properly to interpret them. And we must analyze the concept of a value domain of which the value situation itself is a component. Once these topics have been traversed, I think, the possibilities that exist for a scientific treatment of value on a plan uniquely different from the standard imitation of natural science will be evident, as should what this treatment of value can do to transform our time-honored and current practice in dealing with the problems of value in our culture.

As to the topical or cultural problem, we might indicate very schematically our answer in terms of the results of our systematic study. Human value activities generally, we shall argue, occur in domains: politics, science, art, family life, and so on, each with its own distinctive purpose structure; this purpose structure "defines" the value possibilities and value requirements distinctive of the domain. It includes what unique purpose realizations are possible and can be coherently required within the domain's limits, and thereby it furnishes a special principle of value action and a special principle of value judgment, that is, a principle for judging what is fitting and right and good in the domain in question. Since value activities generally are of the domain sort, the unique problems of human value, the problems of proper purposes or aims, then become amenable to detailed and specialized theoretical treatment. They are set up as problems of rigorous "objective" domain analysis or analysis of areas with distinctive and identifiable structural characteristics, and thus become capable of the kind of approximate and indefinitely corrigible handling familiar in the established sciences. Moreover, as these theoretical inquiries develop and gain in strength and power, they should acquire the same kind of universal and exact application in practice as applications of natural science in technologies. They would require for this a parallel type of institutional embodiment, including a strong place in the educational system, and there would be other similar requirements. Their application, however, would differ in one fundamental respect from the established natural science technologies. Instead of describing how natural material must be manipulated to gain human advantage within the rule of causal laws, this *practica* would describe how human beings must handle themselves to realize the authentic value possibilities in the regions where they try to realize them.

Besides being the basis of an answer to a current question, a systematic study of value problems, such as we shall undertake, can have an interest and importance in its own right. Even if nothing in the ensuing chapters had any special bearing on the value problems of contemporary life, we would feel considerably pleased if what was said helped to clarify some major value terms, to sort out a little the great profusion of recent value theories, to introduce a new and more unified view worth considering and improving, or in some other way carried forward one small useful step the efforts now devoted to systematic value study. No doubt, such intrinsic virtues of our inquiry, if they existed, would be rather special to the field. But they would meet one of the evident demands of human advancement that can be made legitimately in the field, and thus be rewarding on this theoretical level, whatever their consequences for the problems of current existence.

Still, there can be no doubt that especially in our public world today we are confronted with value problems of the greatest urgency. We are now witnessing the breakup of old ways of group life and the slow uncertain growth of new intracontinental and intercontinental communities of people. The rise of new national-isms in Asia and Africa may look like a recapitulation of the post-medieval Euro-American past, as in some general respects it is. But it has this vast difference that it is linked much more closely with the larger community of human beings, both for aid and guidance and for survival and independence; and the ceaseless movement toward a live intercommunity of all peoples pulses within its chaotic beginnings. Our planet is "growing smaller" in the sense that the human family is growing larger and physically and socially closer knit, and coupled with the newer stirrings, this develop-ment has resulted in a magnification of hostility of purpose, aim, and value, in the many places where pre-existing or incipient antagonisms of this sort had already been flourishing.

These pre-existing and incipient antagonisms of which the so-called cold war is one product lie deep in the value presuppositions of the whole modern epoch, particularly in the exaggerated indi-vidualism and the power-directed creativity, previously mentioned, that have won such energetic and unreflective adherence. A kind of unconscious turning in these value directions has been in progress for a long time in the modern period, disguised by ideological slogans and political epithets that pass for thought but do not reach the root of the matter. In most of his basic actions, the human being rarely thinks deeply first, then acts accordingly. Indeed, he rarely thinks deeply on his action at all, usually lacking the intellectual resources—the knowledge of human purpose and the value insights—to do so properly. However, implanted in him is an original "governor" which as "educated" by accepted practice leads him to seek certain values and attempt fruitful action. In our public life in postmedieval times, this steering in the semidark has been accompanied by colossal value conflicts and enormous human waste and wreckage. Something basically wrong has lurked in our culture, deep-down in its institutional fabric, in its orientation and training, leading as if inexorably to mounting disaster.[2] The question now is whether we can further afford this unenlightened and even illiterate mode of action; whether for bare survival, not to mention minimum or maximum gain, we dare remain, in our value considerations, in the unscientific semireflective ruts of the past. The belief behind this book is that this way of doing business is finished, or the great segment of the human race that calls itself civilized may itself be finished. We must try with all means in our power, practical as well as cognitive, by skillful statesmanship as well as systematic science and philosophy, to find a better way than we have been following. In particular, "what we need now are human sciences—to educate people how to live in this new world and how to develop social inventions that will make it possible for us to survive."[3] Skillful statesmanship will help, its compromises staving off disaster. But a deeper understanding and a scientific enlightenment of purpose, widely diffused, is the best ultimate hope, and the possibility of this in any effective sense is the chief problem of our times that we shall be addressing.

---

[2] Gotshalk, *The Promise of Modern Life,* Chaps. III, IV.
[3] Margaret Mead in *As We Are,* by Henry Brandon (Garden City, N.Y.: Doubleday & Co., Inc., 1961), p. 33.

CONTENTS

I

THE VALUE SITUATION

Features

What are the features or components of the situation in which human values ordinarily occur? Unquestionably, there are many types of such situations. But I believe any type can be analyzed into at least three components. You feel a cool breeze on a warm sticky day and experience a moment of relief and bodily pleasure. In this situation, there are (1) an object component: the cooling breeze, (2) a subject component: your reactions to the breeze including the feelings of relief and bodily pleasure, and (3) a relational component: the appetitive pattern arising in the subject but extending to the object, indeed in the present instance, excited by the object, if we assume you were not seeking the breeze and that it and the relief it provided were "gratuitous." This appetitive pattern directs the subject's reactions to the breeze, and grades both subject and object components.

Other examples exhibit a generically similar triad of elements. With the aid of others you complete a certain task, such as winning the election of a candidate for political office. Here there are (1) you and your friends, and your activities and theirs: a subject component, (2) the obstacles and other "things" to which all of you applied your activities: an object component, and (3) the purpose pattern directing the activities to the winning and grading them and its objects as factors in this outcome. Or, shifting to a highly "inward" situation, suppose a person is "wrestling" with his conscience concerning an action he is thinking of taking. There are here (1) the person with the anxiety, guilt, doubt, or uncertainty being felt regarding the action: a subject component, (2) the action-as-being-contemplated: an object component, and (3) the ideal of action being applied by the conscience to the contemplated action and grading the value quality of the action as well as the value quality of the states of the subject: a relational component.

Obviously, the terms "subject," "object," "relational," as we plan to use them, will require some further preliminary specification as well as detailed discussion. But obviously also, these three terms in some sense yet to be specified do denote three very prominent features of an individual value situation. However, they do not cover all of the features of the situation, and, before proceeding, let me draw attention to two others, which at this stage may be regarded as background, but which will be of greater importance in later stages of our discussion.

The first is that value situations, even the most trivial of those above described, occur within a social framework or within a setting of traditions, customs, laws, institutions. A value subject is not a self-inclosed substance. Born into a family, acquiring a whole network of relations in the family not merely to people but to things and especially to ways of using things including words, developing a larger if in many cases a more tenuous fabric of connections in neighborhood, school, church, community, even the "immature" individual, as the mature citizen, has had a considerable schooling in the patterns of a culture. And whether his actions extend, modify, or replace some of these folk ways, they always operate within a great many of them, individualizing them and even sometimes catching something of their "color." Later on, we shall mark this fact by saying that value activities and situations occur within domains, and exist as factors of domains, and are exposed to the scrutiny of the domain perspective. We shall also see then that domains essentially are established subject-object patterns, supported in various ways by public agencies and properties. Hence, an analysis here undertaken of the subject-object pattern along with the components of this pattern promises also to take us to the heart of the social background of the value situation itself.

The second feature of this situation that appears at this stage as properly background is the cosmological setting of human action. The human being lives in a society, but a society exists in the universe, and in being a member of society the human being is an inhabitant of the universe. Since the problem we have set ourselves to explore, however, is the problem of human values, a consideration of the cosmic aspects of value will be largely incidental and subordinate. Some of these larger problems can be neglected. For example, the anxiety of the individual concerning his being in Eternity, described by certain existentialists, raises broad questions of cosmological fact and destiny. But it is sufficient for our purpose to consider such anxiety, if at all, as merely illustrating a human value situation, rather than as raising far-reaching questions about the nature and destiny of the universe. Some larger cosmological considerations, however, seem unavoidable. Fundamental discussions of human action can hardly neglect basic concepts such as causality and teleology. Again, a principle of human value raises the question of whether it may be denied or re-enforced by the cosmic layout, or by cosmic prospects. Considerations such as these will find some place in our account, but still will remain primarily incidental to the main discussion.

With these remarks on two background aspects of the value situation, let us return to the three foreground features previously illustrated and give them some further preliminary specification.

The Object Component

Ralph Barton Perry has defined value as an object of any interest.[1] Perry's definition has serious limitations, as we shall see. But it does suggest that value has an object status, that it is not merely subjective, and in this suggestion,[2] I think, it is unquestionably correct. Also, the ascription of value to objects, I believe, must be taken in the most literal sense. By an object I shall mean any item— quality, event, thing, relation, state of mind, or complex of these, actual or possible, past, present, or future—toward which a telic pattern is directed. Such an item has value, where it has value, in the strictest sense. Thus, I contemplate a painting on a wall. I may

---

[1] R. B. Perry, *General Theory of Value* (Cambridge: Harvard University Press, 1926, 1954), pp. 115-116.

[2] It is only a suggestion, for, as we shall argue later, Perry's theory is actually a type of subjectivism.

do this in several ways. I may consider the painting in relation to a purpose assumed or known to have been a factor in its creation. I may consider the painting in relation to a purpose assumed to be valid for any painting. Or, I may consider the painting in terms of my personal desires and aesthetic interests independent of any larger claims. Suppose I contemplate the painting in all three ways, and in each case find it "excellent." The property "excellent"—here a shorthand term for the diverse totality of aesthetic values of the work—is not a property of myself, or the valuing subject. That is, it is not I but the painting that is considered excellent. An objective value, we might say, speaking tentatively and provisionally, consists in the adequacy of an object to the demands of a telic pattern. At least, if an object does show such adequacy, if a food for example satisfies the demand of a hunger drive, as a work of art satisfies the demand of an aesthetic interest, we incline to describe it as having value in this respect. If this is so, then an objective value clearly is found by the valuing subject and not made. In the case of the painting, I discover the adequacy (or not) of the painting, and unless I am mistaken, as I might easily be, as through a misunderstanding of various matters—the object, the purposes of its creation, the purposes of painting, and the like—this property of the painting is a discovery anyone can make for himself, if he will accurately contemplate the object in terms of the telic patterns I have employed in contemplating it.

In the preceding section, we noted that the value activities of human beings occur within a social structure and exist in domains. This is equally true of the object side of the value situation. Thus, to illustrate from objects so far mentioned: the painting on the wall is an item in the field of fine art, a domain with its own purpose structure and requirements. As an excellent painting it may also be an article of economic value, and an important part of a household's furnishings, and it may further be a historical document and an educational aid, placing it in the domains of economics, home life, history, and education. Again, the action being contemplated by the conscience-troubled person, the "things" worked on by the election-winning persons, even the cool breeze, all described above as object components of situations, are connected with domains of general scope. The action is contemplated as a possibility in the domain of moral conduct, the "things" are phenomena in politics, and the cool breeze, even as a free gift of nature, is an item in the health-recreation domain, at least as described above. In sum, objects as human value objects, no less than human beings, fit into larger value-patterns in the very role of being objects of individual human purpose. But the further discussion of this, and of domains and of the relation of domains to a science of value, will be given later.

The Subject Component

The term "subject" has numerous meanings, but primarily, and in the present instance, by subject or the subject component of the value situation will be meant the human being or beings in that situation in whom is rooted the telic pattern being directed to the object. Ordinarily, the subject component in this sense is an organism with all its activities and states, engaged with some extrabodily object, for example, a painting, a cool breeze, and so forth. But there are some exceptions to this, two particularly, which should be mentioned to make clear the primary meaning of subject as used in our discussion.

The first occurs in instances of self-examination, situations in which the object is the person's own thoughts, plans, actions, feelings, body, or bodily parts. Here the subject is the psychophysical individual as directing attention to the object in question. The peculiar characteristic of this situation is that the object is "internal" to the person who is the subject. This seeming paradox is explained by the fact of self-consciousness which implies that a person or self can be an object or end-point of interest and attention for its own self, and that the usual subject-external object paradigm, characteristic of ordinary transactions as well as of animal life, does not cover all situations of human beings. It is true that the object here is usually some possession—quality, intent, action—of the person, not the whole self in all the details it might be known to have by a "perfect" Knower. But in principle there is no reason why this object may not be all the self or at least all the principles of its being or any amount in between, provided this amount can be brought into self-consciousness and become the focus of purposive self-conscious attention.

The second exception occurs in cases where groups are considered as the subject component of a situation, as in law a corporation may be considered a person. This procedure seems particularly appropriate where a group is united by a single purpose and operating on a related set of objects: a musical quartet, a scientific team, a pressure group, a political party. To treat these as the subject pole of a situation provides not only an easy way to discuss very complex situations, but also a fairly realistic way, since groups of the sort just mentioned are more than the sum of their parts taken additively. Of course, where such groups are divided in purpose, where they are fraught with conflict and antagonism, the best way to under-stand them is to take them apart, that is, to resolve them into their multiple factions. These factional subgroups then become subjects in diverse telic relations to objects and with objects compose situa-tions that are clear separately but are confused when taken as a single situation. The justification for treating a group in certain cases as a subject is that, in the respect in which a group is as united in purpose as an individual, there is no difference in principle between it and an individual, so far as value posture goes. Also, in so many of our value actions the individual really is serving as a representa-tive of a group: that is, he is representing the purpose of the group. Hence, the transition from the individual seeking his own purpose and a group seeking its, is not a leap from one entity to another entirely different, but a transition between entities that shade into each other and are of the same general kind so far as their role in the value configuration is concerned.

J. R. Reid has defined value as "given affective quality."[3] This definition, I believe, does not describe value but merely a fragment of the subject component of the value situation. But the definition is typical of many efforts to locate value in the subject area. Such efforts, as we shall see, fail in their main aim, which is to reduce value exclusively or primarily to subjective terms. Yet they are important in emphasizing that value is a property of subjects, as it is also a property of objects, and that an analysis of value must be wide enough to include this.

Let me illustrate in a preliminary way some aspects of this fact. And to do this properly, I think, we must go immediately beyond "given affective quality." Thus, a great many subjective processes occur, vegetative, animal, subconscious, which analysis shows em-body telic patterns. In these processes, there may be no given affective quality in the sense of consciously felt pleasure, and the

---

[3] J. R. Reid, *A Theory of Value* (New York: Charles Scribner's Sons, 1938), p. 54.

like. Yet such processes, for example, a good dead-to-the-world sleep, may fulfill ends and be of value to the being of the subject. Moreover, limiting subjective value even on the conscious level to given affective quality or specifically to positive affective quality, "pleasure" or "pleasantness," seems a mistake. This is enjoyment value. But the human organism does much more than enjoy. For example, it creates. It is a system that not only is modified by the environment but also modifies the environment. There are the achievements of creation as well as the pleasures of enjoyment. One might liken the enjoyments of satisfactory aesthetic experience to the affective element of subjective value. There is more to aesthetic experience than that, I think, but, where it is satisfying, surely that. The contrast then would be with the realizations of the artist in successful creative activity. In this, the object is not so much enjoyed as molded to the purpose of the creator, so that this purpose may be fulfilled in the object. Of course, the fulfillment if it occurs may be enjoyed, as it is occurring or afterward. But the fulfillment is analytically distinct from the enjoyment. Indeed, a person may fulfill a creative urge and in the ordinary sense not enjoy it at all. He may create in torment. Yet, simply as fulfillment, the process may mark an addition to his stature as a creative being and so be of subjective value.

The Relational Component

Generally, the relational component consists of the telic pattern governing a value situation. This pattern, which we shall analyze in a moment, originates in the subject but extends to the object, uniting it with the subject into a value situation. Hence, it is not in any of the above senses strictly subjective nor strictly objective. It is tied into both ends of the situation and is the link between the two. Moreover, of all components, it is, I believe, the most fundamental for the situation as a value situation. Eliminate it, and as we shall see, subjects have no principle for grading their possessions or processes, while objects have nothing against which to exhibit the adequacies that constitute their values as human objects. In other words, the human value situation collapses and is turned into a situation in which things happen in a mechanically connected way, but no principle of human value, subjective or objective, can be found.

Any telic pattern can be analyzed into two main factors. To

confine the analysis here to the individual level, although it applies equally, with minor qualifications, to domains and the social level, there is always, first of all, a telic factor, or at a minimum, some drive, need, want, impulse, urge, desire, appetition, propensity, interest, aim, purpose, or other directional element. In addition, there is a set of requirements, stemming from the telic factor and placed upon the object, that is, upon some quality, relation, action, state, event, thing, or complex of these, actual or possible, past, present, or future, toward which the aim or *telos* is directed. I shall call this set of requirements the vector factor.[4]

So far as the object side of the situation is concerned, the vector of the pattern is its chief element. This vector consists of a group of demands or requirements set up by the aim as directed to the object. In consequence, within the aim pursued, it determines the area of relevant objects and the relevant values of these objects in the value situation. Thus, to use an example from the area of "practical" action, if I want to catch a train and am told that the moon is or is not made of green cardboard, this information may or may not be interesting in a vague sort of way, but it is unlikely to seem very relevant or very valuable at the time, particularly if I have not a moment to spare. Prove to me, however, that my train is ten minutes late—introduce this different objective element (information about the train's lateness) into the situation—and the matter is otherwise. This information intersects vividly with the vector in the situation, which contains among other things the requirement that my train be at the station at a convenient time. As a result, the information seems immediately relevant and important.

On the subject side of the situation, the telic factor is of more direct moment. As the vector grades the objects or object elements of a situation, so the purpose or other telic factor guides and grades the operations, realizations, and enjoyments of the subject. For example, I wish to perform some simple act, such as lighting a fire in a stove. My purpose here directs the operations constituting the act, and measures the value of the operations, their relevance, aptness, and the like, and the value of the realizations and enjoyments, if any, that I gain through these operations. I evaluate my

---

[4] Cf. Wolfgang Köhler, *The Place of Value in a World of Facts* (New York: Liveright Publishing Corp., 1938).

actions by my purpose. Usually, however, simple telic factors do not occur in isolation but in combination. In lighting the fire, I may also have other purposes in mind: to get warm, to boil water, to prepare coffee, to provide refreshments for a friend, all of which may enter into the evaluating process. Or, a contrary purpose may seize me, devaluating my present acts, and I may blow out the lighted match and proceed to business elsewhere. Such concomitant or sequent purposes may be linked into many arrangements: hierarchical, serial, antithetical, evolutionary. Moreover, in addition to abstract formal order, these diverse purposes, as telic factors in mature individual agents or subjects, tend to exhibit certain particularized settled orders. They outline a profile of value tendencies recurring in various guises in various situations.

To anticipate the argument slightly, one might call the totality of telic factors in an agent, insofar as it exhibits settled outline, the character or personality core of the agent, personality differing from character only as including an admixture of inherited traits such as temperament. There are well-knit personalities whose every purpose seems to radiate from a single center. There are personalities, perhaps more numerous, whose purposes do not seem at times to be on very intimate terms with each other, exhibiting a persistent and sometimes disastrous incoherence. But whatever the qualities of such totalities, single telic factors of a mature agent, as they enter into telic patterns organizing value situations, usually are connected like tiny shoots with a larger telic mass, which incidentally serves as a kind of supreme court of personal or subjective value, abrogating the authority of certain single telic factors and giving to others a kind of unexpected strength that by themselves they do not and sometimes should not have.

Other Situations

The foregoing preliminary discussion of value components is concerned only with positive situations. It omits all negative situations, or ones in which disvalues occur.

Such situations are numerous, but I believe introduce no new principles. Thus, a person may view a work of art not with pleasure but with keen disappointment. Here there are (1) the subject or person who is viewing the work and experiencing the disappointment with its unpleasant affective quality, (2) the work of art, the object, and (3) the telic pattern maintained by the subject and placing demands on the object. Such situations may have positive values, for example, be instructive about the deficiencies of a certain artist. But taken at their face value, as experiences of disappointment (subjective) or of deficiency (objective), they are merely the situations previously described with negative values in place of positive at the subject and/or object poles.

A variant of positive situations possessing certain negative features has also been omitted, namely, aversions. A person may shun an object that is threatening or distasteful to him, such as a violent thunderstorm. A successful aversion I think involves the usual tripartite setup of positive and negative situations, but in details the components are somewhat different. As in a negative situation, the object has disvalue or a disvalue. But this disvalue arouses a telic pattern in which the purpose is to achieve avoidance or flight, and the vector is a demand on the situation for circumstances permitting avoidance or flight. The successful execution of this pattern is a positive achievement with concomitant enjoyment values of relief or with "neutral" enjoyment values. Thus, while aversions differ in detail from both positive and negative value situations and exhibit a complex medley of factors, they fall well within the triadic outline of the value situation we have given.

Plan

This triadic outline of the value situation, as I have said, assumes a cosmological setting within which such situations occur, and a complex social framework with its numerous domains within which value situations fit often in multiple ways. With these assumptions, I think, it opens up a field for the analysis of value that is broad enough to enable us to reach at least a well-grounded tentative decision on the main topical problem before us about the possibility of a new scientific treatment of values.

Traditionally, the analysis of value has been centered around the concept of the good life, and in many respects this concept is a satisfactory point for centering it. On such a plan, what we would need to indicate chiefly are the range and content of the fields of subjective and objective values, and the meaning of the principle of value with some incidental attention to the social structure and cosmic setting of human beings. Such a discussion would delineate in our terms a general concept of the good life, or at least, its materials and principle. We shall have something to say on the concept of the good life in our final chapter. But to consider the possibility of a new scientific treatment of values and of a system of new value sciences, something more is needed. Of course, we shall want to investigate the varieties of value, the value principle, and its bearings on the social structure and cosmic setting. But we shall also want to discuss value knowledge and domains, the nature of science and of value science.

This plan is not meant to suggest that we intend to concentrate on highly technical aspects of value and neglect common concerns. On the contrary, our whole view is that the main value problem of our times arises from our common life, and the solution of it is to be applied there. Also, a connection with ordinary experience is intended throughout all the discussion to follow. Thus, we have said that the principle of value itself is the telic pattern or relational component in the value situation. Now, the clue to this view can readily be found in ordinary experience when people say this or that is good. When people say that this food, drink, weather, radio or TV program is good, I believe they mean, among other things, that the food or drink or whatever comes up to a certain standard or set of demands placed upon it. It satisfies the vector of a telic pattern, to speak the language already used. In the ensuing discussions of the principle of value, we shall follow up this clue, trying to free its concept in ordinary experience from evident imperfections and to show how it can be developed into a self-sustaining value principle.

In recent times much has been made of ordinary experience and usage in value discussion, although some of the conclusions reached are not in agreement with our own views. This is particularly true regarding the problem of value knowledge. Indeed, here a number of philosophers, some classified as ordinary-language philosophers, have denied a knowledge claim to value statements. They assert that value statements in ordinary experience, and in philosophy also, for example, "This X (food) is good" or "X (pleasure) is good," have no descriptive meaning, only emotive, prescriptive, or other meaning. Value statements express attitudes, not beliefs or knowledge. A good deal of this recent discussion has been used to portray various roles of language, or, as they are sometimes called, various logical properties of language, and has resulted in such a proliferation of detail as often to black out substantive problems and to give much recent philosophical discourse on ethical questions and value theory, an unfortunately scholastic and sterile quality far removed from the lively concerns of ordinary mortals. However, the problem of the knowledge claim of value statements and the problem of value knowledge are sharply relevant to the question of the possibility of a scientific treatment of value, forming a kind of first hurdle in the consideration of this problem. In consequence, we shall proceed at once to this problem, discussing it in such detail as seems necessary for our purpose.

II
KNOWLEDGE

General Position

In one sense, this book as a whole is an effort to show by argument and example that knowledge of values is possible. What we shall try to do in this chapter is to state a general position and enlarge on certain aspects of it. In some respects, therefore, the argument of the chapter will remain incomplete. But it is hoped that the necessary missing details will be adequately supplied by discussions in other chapters, notably "Domains" (VI) and "Sciences" (VII).

At the outset, let us be clear on one point. When we refer to "knowledge of values" we do not mean merely or primarily knowledge of what people have valued, or do or probably will value. There is plenty of such knowledge. Anthropology, history, psychology, and sociology can supply it in great quantity, and no one commonly disputes, or at least we shall not dispute, that this information on these topics is knowledge. But, accurately speaking, this information is knowledge about people, not about values. Distinctive knowledge of value, if any, is information about the right and good, the ought and the should be, not about what people have held, or do hold, or will hold to be right or good, the ought to be or the should be.

Our general position is that distinctive knowledge about the right and good, about norms and principles of evaluation, is capable of genuine empirical discovery, and of scientific development. In the field of value theory, this view is the exact opposite of a thesis of certain logical empiricists who hold that only statements describing what people have valued, or do or will value, have empirical or scientific standing. Only descriptive anthropological, psychological, and sociological generalizations or reports are admissible by empirical method, while all other statements, particularly regarding principles of evaluation, norms, the ought or should be, are merely expressions of private emotion and prejudice, and have no cognitive, empirical, or scientific standing or validity.

The paradox of this noncognitivist thesis is fairly obvious, for the thesis is really a *thesis*, not a synopsis. That is, it is an assertion not of what people generally value, have valued, or will value as knowledge (this is exceedingly various), but of what logical positivists believe they ought to value or should rightly value as knowledge. It is a statement of an ought or should be. Hence, in self-consistency the thesis itself cannot claim any empirical, scientific, or cognitive standing, and can be set aside as merely one more expression of private emotion and prejudice.

But the root of the difficulty, I believe, lies elsewhere, in a faulty conception of experience. According to this view, experience is sensory apprehension. It is awareness of sensory presentations, sense data, or sensa. This conception is combined with the view that all knowledge that is not analytic consists of statements, such as psychological and sociological statements, the content of which is allegedly reducible to descriptions of past, present, or future sense data. Even omitting the numerous sophisticated preplexities of the sense-datum concept, this view has an elementary fatal difficulty. It omits the telic structure of experience. It conceives experience as mechanical, a mere recording of the "given"; whereas experience in its major modes is an apprehension of the given in terms of need, purposes, and goals.

The experience of the physical scientist himself—the paragon knower for the positivist—illustrates this. A physicist wishes to make a measurement. Of the thousand and one possible combinations of data that a free sensibility might record when it is directed toward a clock or a measuring rod, the physicist concentrates on one combination, for example, the positions of the hands of the clock or the incidence points of the ends of the measuring rod. Why?

Obviously, because this combination is to his purpose. Similarly, in preparing and conducting an experiment, the physicist sets up and manipulates his object field in terms of an aim. If the aim requires that certain items appear and operate in the object field and no others, these items are introduced and arranged there, and the others are controlled, so far as possible, as the aim requires. Both in observation and experiment, experience in physical science contains ordering purposes and goals. What is, is caught within a network of oughts and should-bes springing from telic demands.

As a matter of fact, when logical positivists themselves discuss science, they often speak, as in value theory, of oughts and should bes, of demands and requirements. Thus, Carnap writes: "It is a just demand that Science should have not merely subjective interpretation but sense and validity for all subjects who participate in it."[1] Either this statement is merely an expression of private emotion and prejudice, and so empirical and scientific nonsense, or it is a serious recognition that science and scientific experience contain universal imperatives and goals, since it demands that would-be scientific statements measure up to certain requirements of sense and validity in the experience of all who participate in science. I conclude, what seems clear anyway from the example of the physical scientist cited above, that ought and should be, demands and requirements, as springing from purposes, aims, and goals, are internal to experience and not outside it, and therefore that statements about them are in principle open to empirical examination and testing in the sense that they can be confronted by evidence based on an element of experience itself.

Ordinary Experience

In everyday life, particularly on its active or practical side, value statements typified by "This is good" constantly occur, and in this burgeoning century of the common man, philosophers have been busy trying to determine what these statements mean. Philosophers have come to various conclusions. As just indicated, positivists and logical empiricists, such as Carnap, and also Reichenbach, Russell, and Ayer, have decided that such statements are emotive expres-

---

[1] Rudolph Carnap, *Unity of Science*, Eng. trans. (London: Kegan Paul, 1938), p. 66.

sions which have no cognitive content.[2] The statements say nothing about fact or what is the case, only express and/or seek to arouse emotion about it. According to Charles L. Stevenson, "This is good" means "I approve of this; do so as well!"[3] That is, the statement expresses an emotion of approval coupled with an enjoinder on others of approval. A large group of other philosophers, representing a tendency sometimes called informalism or the philosophy of ordinary language,[4] finds a multitude of other meanings or uses in ordinary value statements. Besides expressing emotion, or specifically, approval, according to these philosophers, value terms such as "good," "right," in everyday contexts, are used to exhort, to advise, to recommend, to prescribe a course of action or way of life, to ascribe a function or obligation, to perform an act, to carry authority in the manner of certain kinds of ceremonial utterances. Ordinary value statements function as exhortatory,[5] advisory or commendatory,[6] prescriptive,[7] ascriptive,[8] performatory,[9] and ceremonial.[10]

Now, in everyday life, particularly in predominantly "practical"

[2] Rudolph Carnap, *Philosophy and Logical Syntax* (London: Kegan Paul, 1935), pp. 23-25; Hans Reichenbach, "Philosophy: Speculation or Science," in *The Nation*, Vol. CLXIV (1947), pp. 19-22. Bertrand Russell, *Religion and Science* (London: T. Butterworth, 1935; New York: Oxford University Press [Galaxy Book], 1961), pp. 230-243; Alfred J. Ayer, *Language, Truth and Logic*, 2nd ed. (London: Victor Gollancz, Ltd., 1946), pp. 20-22, 107-114.

[3] Charles L. Stevenson, *Ethics and Language* (New Haven, Conn.: Yale University Press, 1944), p. 21.

[4] Philip B. Rice, *On the Knowledge of Good and Evil* (New York: Random House, Inc., 1955), p. 74.

[5] P. H. Nowell-Smith, *Ethics* (London: Penguin Books, 1954), p. 158.

[6] R. M. Hare, *The Language of Morals* (Oxford: Clarendon Press, 1952), pp. 127 ff.

[7] Stuart Hampshire, "Fallacies in Moral Philosophy," *Mind*, Vol. 58 (1948), pp. 466-482.

[8] H. L. A. Hart, "The Ascription of Responsibility and Rights," in *Logic and Language*, 1st ser., ed. by A. G. N. Flew (New York: The Philosophical Library, 1951).

[9] J. L. Austin, "Other Minds," in *Logic and Language*, 2nd ser., ed. by A. G. N. Flew (New York: The Philosophical Library, 1953).

[10] Margaret Macdonald, "Ethics and the Ceremonial Uses of Language," in *Philosophical Analysis*, ed. by Max Black (Ithaca, N.Y.: Cornell University Press, 1950), pp. 211-229.

situations, value statements may have any one, several, and in some contexts, all of these meanings or uses. Moreover, these meanings may be the chief or primary ones of the statements there. Confronted with a question about a proposed course of action, A may say to his friend B, "In my opinion, that course of action is the good one." And everyday situations and the motives of people being as complex as they are, this statement in the context may serve primarily to advise, recommend, exhort, prescribe, or express approval and a general pro attitude. Or, with a slight change of tone or circumstances, the statement may serve to ascribe an obligation, or carry ceremonial authority. Furthermore, since such statements in everyday life occur usually in situations demanding action or are uttered in connection with action, the statement may itself be the action wanted or may serve to incite to further action or at least have a gerundive function,[11] pointing out what is to be done. Certainly, the above statement would not be intended to convey, nor would it convey, any natural science knowledge, and have in this sense a cognitive function. Finally, all of this may be true of most value statements in everyday life when they are seen realistically in their practical context, where the pressures for action tend to outweigh other considerations and give these statements an overwhelmingly practical and noncognitive role.

Nevertheless, these concessions do not quite clinch the point. A cognitive function of a certain sort may still be imbedded in such statements. In propaganda, advertising, or verbal activity intended to deceive or merely to arouse emotion, a cognitive element of any sort may be purely illusory. But in the run of everyday statements, made sincerely, to advise, exhort, and so forth, I think it is otherwise. Thus when A says sincerely to his friend B: "In my opinion that course of action is the good one," he means that he approves it, advises it, and the like, but he also usually means that in his opinion the course of action in the circumstances conforms to some standard of a good action he (A) has in mind, that it is adequate to evident demands of this standard (e.g., it is honest or financially feasible or politically effective or whatever), and that the action has this adequacy as a property. And the more outspoken his opinion of the course of action is, or the more he is asked why

---

[11] Stephen Toulmin, *An Examination of the Place of Reason in Ethics* (Cambridge: Cambridge University Press, 1950), pp. 70-74.

he thinks as he does, the more explicit these beliefs will become. In such beliefs, A may be wrong. The action may not conform to his standard. Or, the standard itself may not satisfy the requirements of a good standard for judging the action, and so conformity to it may not be proof that the action is a good one. But the very fact that A may be wrong implies that A could be right, that correct belief or knowledge of a value property in the situation is possible. And it is this fact—the possibility of value knowledge not its actuality nor indeed the multiple functions of value language which no one need deny—that is the important point in the present connection.

In "everyday" statements, one might grant, even emphasize, that the cognitive element is usually a relatively minor component, for the most part not too explicitly developed, while the intent to advise, incite, and in general, the emotive and volitional meanings, usually have great prominence. Everyday practical situations are primarily action situations, not cognitive, and ordinarily the leading role of language here is to incite or suspend or deter action, not to be a vehicle of knowledge. The point is merely that a cognitive element is usually *also* included in ordinary everyday appraisals, and that ordinary appraisal statements, made sincerely, usually involve a belief about the adequacy (or inadequacy) of an action, a subject, an object, or other item. No doubt, such beliefs often may be not only incidental but also hasty, misleading, mistaken, and generally, of inferior cognitive quality. Yet they *are* beliefs, they make cognitive claims, and, in certain cases, where common wisdom shows itself at its best, they seem to make clearly valid cognitive claims. In this sense, they are evidence, from the most practical noncontemplative action level, where language flourishes in multiple noncognitive ways, that value knowledge of some type or sort is certainly possible.[12]

We might note here, in passing, that among positivists, emotivists, and some philosophers of ordinary language, there has prevailed the very curious conception that philosophical writings on value, as distinct from value statements in ordinary life, are efforts to persuade, exhort, influence emotionally or volitionally, in the manner of ordinary language or of a speaker in an everyday practical

---

[12] Cf. Richard B. Brandt, *Ethical Theory* (Englewood Cliffs, N.J.: Prentice-Hall, Inc., 1959), p. 241.

situation. For example, the assertion "This is good," as stated by a father to his son or by a philosopher in a treatise where "this" equals "pleasure," has been taken to be the same kind of statement, with the same kind of meaning, and yielding to the same type of analysis. Now, no doubt, an element of persuasion and a desire to influence have entered into the writings of philosophers from Plato and Aristotle through Santayana and Dewey to the positivists and emotivists themselves. Nor I might add is this element absent from the present work. But the main aim and function of philosophical writings on value surely have been to describe the nature, varieties, and principles of value, as the philosophers have understood them. That is, the main aim has been cognitive—to provide a description and understanding of values. Even such a statement as the positivist's: "values are mere subjective prejudices," makes at least such a cognitive claim, that is, the claim to be a true statement about values. The multifunctionality of language allows a multiproportionality between its different functions, specifically its cognitive and noncognitive functions. In this regard, philosophy in value analysis inverts practical life wherein cognition tends to be incidental and instrumental only, and emotional-volitional influence to be primary. Philosophy seeks to study and describe the diverse meanings and types and aspects of value, and while sometimes a philosopher may advance the misconception that ordinary value statements, like philosophical ones, are primarily cognitive, this misconception—as witness the positivist and emotivist philosophers—is no necessary part or implication of philosophy itself in the study of values.

Meanwhile, the general position we have taken in regard to value knowledge is obviously incomplete, open to misinterpretation, and easily confused with certain other fundamentally different positions. We return, therefore, to our main topic, and first to some remarks about recent intuitionism.

Intuition

Our view stated in the preceding section that value knowledge is possible, that it consists, among other things, of knowledge of a quality "good" and that this quality is not a property described by natural science, suggests a theory of value knowledge outlined by G. E. Moore in *Principia Ethica* (1903) following Sidgwick, which has come to be known as intuitionism. According to Moore, the answer to the question "What is good?" is that good is a simple and indefinable quality belonging to things, and the knowledge expressed in this proposition is intuitive in the sense of being incapable of proof or disproof. In support of propositions ascribing this kind of simple intrinsic goodness to things "no relevant evidence whatever can be adduced: from no other truth, except themselves alone, can it be inferred that they are either true or false." In order to express the fact that value propositions of this type are their own warrant and "are incapable of proof or disproof" by other truths, Moore states, "I have sometimes followed Sidgwick's usage in calling them 'Intuitions.'"[13] This doctrine that basic value properties and propositions are self-evident has been extended by W. D. Ross to include propositions about duties or the right,[14] and is held with various modifications by other writers, notably, C. D. Broad and A. C. Ewing.[15]

This recent intuitionism has been criticized on many points. Its characterization of good as a non-natural quality has been shown to be vague and confused.[16] Its description of good as simple and indefinable has been shown to rest on a restricted theory of definition that conceives definition as an enumeration of parts of extensive wholes. The crucial conception of intuitive certainty, or self-evidence, likened by Ross to the self-evidence of a mathematical axiom,[17] has been generally disputed, not merely because of the rejection of such alleged certainties in mathematics and in natural science, but also because what seems self-evident to one intuitionist apparently is not self-evident to another. And there have been

---

[13] G. E. Moore, *Principia Ethica* (Cambridge: Cambridge University Press, 1903, 1954), pp. viii-x.

[14] W. D. Ross, *The Right and the Good* (Oxford: Clarendon Press, 1930), p. 29.

[15] C. D. Broad, *Five Types of Ethical Theory* (London: Routledge & Kegan Paul, Ltd., 1930); A. C. Ewing, *The Definition of Good* (New York: Macmillan Co., 1947).

[16] G. E. Moore, himself, in reply to his critics, admits that his (earlier) view of natural and non-natural qualities was "silly and preposterous," without adding much to amend it. See *The Philosophy of G. E. Moore*, ed. by P. A. Schilpp (Evanston, Ill.: Northwestern University Press, 1942).

[17] W. D. Ross, *The Right and the Good*, p. 29.

numerous additional criticisms.[18] It should be already clear also that the theory of value knowledge we have been outlining implies certain criticisms of the intuitionist view. According to our theory, good as a quality is not indefinable. It can be defined in terms of adequacy to a standard. Moreover, propositions about it are not self-evident in the sense that no relevant evidence whatever for them can be adduced, for often the adequacy that defines good as a quality (e.g., the good of a medicine) is not even plausible, not to say certain, unless knowledge of various other properties of the object is set forth (e.g., chemical properties), or the standard by which the object is adjudged good is shown to meet the requirements of a good standard in this particular area.

Despite its many difficulties, and its divergences from our own views, I believe recent intuitionism has certain clear merits, and contains tenets or suggestions of tenets that are correct. Its view that value is an objective quality or quality of objects, according to the preceding chapter, is true as a description of one type of value. Its theory that value as an objective quality is non-natural, while vague and misleading, seems also correct in one respect. Our own view, it is true, implies that value as an objective quality may be a quality of a natural object as of other objects (however "natural" is defined), since objective value is *prima facie* a quality of any object that is adequate to an appropriate telic demand, and a "natural" object in any reasonable meaning clearly may be among the objects that meet such demands. If the intuitionist doctrine is meant to deny this, its view that value is a non-natural quality seems mistaken. Nevertheless, value as a quality of objects, even of natural objects, is not such a property as mass or gravity, that appears in the equations of the physical sciences in their characteristic effort to formulate causal laws. If one means by a non-natural quality "not a value or a variable used by physical science in its

[18] Cf. Rice, *On the Knowledge of Good and Evil*, Chap. 2; R. B. Perry, *General Theory of Value* (Cambridge: Harvard University Press, 1926), pp. 28 ff.; Nowell-Smith, *Ethics,* Chap. 3; Moritz Schlick, *Problems of Ethics* (New York: Prentice-Hall, Inc., 1939), pp. 107 ff.; P. F. Strawson, "Ethical Intuitionism," *Philosophy,* Vol. 24 (1949), reprinted in *Readings in Ethical Theory,* ed. by Wilfrid Sellars and John Hospers (New York: Appleton-Century-Crofts, Inc., 1952), pp. 250-259; K. Baier, *The Moral Point of View* (Ithaca, N.Y.: Cornell University Press, 1958), pp. 22-24; Brandt, *Ethical Theory,* pp. 188-197.

equations to delineate the causal structure of nature," value as an objective quality is non-natural. Of course, value is a property of the human enterprise called physical science, and physical scientists also wish to "see" it in the objects they investigate—for example, they wish to find or construct and study "good" specimens of natural transactions. But "value" or "good" as such is not the focus of physical science investigations. What they seek and study in their available specimens are the physical characteristics and causal patterns of these characteristics, not whether these items—mass, gravity, the laws of thermodynamics—are good or evil.

Perhaps, however, the chief contribution of recent intuitionism to a right conception of value knowledge is its giving a basic position in this knowledge to the immediate, and to direct insight. Some views of intuitionists here are misleading, even wrong, in particular the belief in self-evident propositions incapable of proof or disproof, absolutes of knowledge, alleged by some to be grasped by an *a priori* cognitive power. Some things that we inspect directly, it is true, seem to us self-evidently right or good, and to be necessarily clear to anyone of proper maturity who will take the trouble to see what is to be seen. But unfortunately some people of proper maturity who do take the trouble sometimes do not see these things exactly as we see them. Moreover, any belief about immediately discovered value predicates is always open theoretically if not practically to reassessment. The assumptions of such beliefs, such as assumptions about the nature of objects, about standards of appraisal, about the laws of logic and psychology, are so numerous, and so likely to need some rectification upon reinvestigation of the situation, that the theoretical finality of the beliefs is always capable of being challenged, however little we ourselves may challenge it.

While all of this may shake credence in self-evident value propositions, and absolutes of knowledge incapable of proof, two aspects of the intuitionist doctrine here still retain a certain degree of cogency.

First, relative to any value-knowledge situation, we invariably accept, and must accept, certain principles as "absolutes." At a minimum, in all usual cases, we accept the laws of logic, and beyond these, our assumptions ramify in many often unfathomable directions, from the standard usage of words in our language to fragments of highly personal psychological information, perhaps of ourselves or of a friend, that only we at the particular moment know at all. These cognitions we accept immediately as having the value of knowledge, or as given certainties, it being necessary for us to do so to get to the something else which is the object of investigation. Or, we accept these cognitions "intuitively," without proof, or as self-proving, for indeed if we questioned them or stopped to try to prove them, we would never get to investigate what we intended to investigate in the first place—a situation incidentally prevailing in much ethics and value theory today, where the study of value knowledge in many cases has become so elaborate and Jesuitical that it has sidetracked the study of the ethical life and values themselves.

Second, apart from these "intuitive" cognitions in the value-knowledge situation, tentatively accepted as final, we often proceed to *new* cognitions by a process of direct insight. Thus, we may appraise an act of a friend as right or good by a direct inspection of the act. Such "intuitive" insight, it is true, often is possible only because we bring to the situation a great apparatus of knowledge and standards. But, however grounded in accepted beliefs, this intuition is a direct insight into the value quality of the inspected act. Of course, we do make innumerable appraisals that are inferential, ranging from our usual pronouncements on foreign political affairs to our appraisals of what was in the mind of an ancient philosopher when he wrote certain words. But even in judging such "remote" objects we usually evaluate certain intermediary objects, such as printed reports, and here the cognition of the value quality of these objects may be as direct as the cognition of the value quality of our friend's action. Incidentally, by "direct" here is meant not that the cognition is flawless or infallible, although it may turn out to be, but that the cognition is of a quality of an item present to the subject, and not of the item as past or future or elsewhere.

This general point is rather important, since there is a curious belief in certain quarters—notably among pragmatists—that all value knowledge is prediction or assertion about the future.[19] Taking an example very favorable to this view, to say as an expert might: "This golf stick is good" means that if you use the stick properly, you will get excellent results or consequences of an ad-

---

[19] Cf. C. I. Lewis, *The Analysis of Knowledge and Valuation* (La Salle, Ill.: Open Court Publishing Co., 1946).

vantageous sort. The evaluation is a prediction, a forecast of consequences, a description about the stick in the future. This view of value knowledge seems singularly incomplete, even for such cases as the one under consideration. Thus, the golf expert may have made the quoted statement just *after* using the golf stick, and the statement may summarize an observation of a value or set of values displayed and directly apprehended in the present-just-passed. Or, before using it, the expert may have examined the golf stick carefully, making his statement then. In that case, it would be a summary of his present observation of the present size, shape, weight, handling ease, and similar characteristics of the object as they fit into his preformed ideal of a good golf stick. In other words, depending on the context, the quoted statement may imply or sum up a good deal of value information about the stick in the present-just-passed, or in the present of observation. Of course, in the case of a usable instrument, such as a golf stick, the statement has implications for the future. It means that, in the future, under certain conditions, certain consequences should follow. But the point is that it does not necessarily mean *only* that. And it may not primarily mean that at all. It may mean primarily a good deal about the present, and even a good deal about the past. Moreover, it is important to note that the confirmations of the statement provided by the future must themselves rest upon a kind of direct knowing. We observe these consequences in a present, now future, and it is by a process of intuitive or direct cognition—of directly witnessing the congruence of the consequences with the expectations set up by the statement—that we confirm the statement, and gain what value knowledge of the object we do gain in the now present future.

This comment on a tenet of pragmatism is not intended as an assessment of that doctrine as a theory of knowledge. Pragmatism has taken many forms, has numerous tenets, and has made many contributions to our understanding of knowledge, including value knowledge. Notably, pragmatism has revitalized traditional empiricism, lifted it out of the rut of a static and mechanical sense-data theory, and imparted to its concept of experience a dynamic character; and it has been especially successful in delineating the knowledge process in terms of purpose, for example, with Dewey, the purpose of problem-solving. Still, whatever its merits, pragmatism has also tended to over-fluxify things, to see everything prospectively, in the forward-looking manner of the "pioneer" mentality. The correction of its futurism, at least in value knowledge, is the doctrine of direct understanding or insight, derived from intuitionism. This suggests a cognitive power capable of apprehending value quality in *present* being, and such a power, as well as prediction, seems implied by the plain meaning of innumerable value-knowledge statements, and indeed by confirmation of prediction itself.

Method

Certain aspects of value knowledge, as we have said, will be discussed later, particularly in the chapters on "Domains" and "Sciences." Perhaps, we can best say what needs to be added at this point by commenting on the method of value theory. Our remarks on informalism, intuitionism, and pragmatism probably have suggested that our chief inclination in methodology is toward empiricism, and this suggestion is correct. But the empiricism that seems to us suitable in the value field is quite different from most doctrines called empiricism in current and traditional Western philosophy, and includes a strong rationalist admixture. In truth, proper method in the value field seems to require a combination of empirical and rational elements. Let me briefly discuss each, beginning with some remarks on experience, that is, value experience.

Human values, it has been our theme, belong in the first instance to the polar components and structure of the value situation: the subject, the object, the tie between the two. If this is the case, then the experience of valuable things, if it occurs, as it obviously does, is more than a mechanical recording of discrete sense data or a Humean registration of separate and unconnected qualities or impressions. This experience must possess a power to apprehend wholes—situations, objects, and subjects as units, not as bits and pieces, while the sensory powers in terms of which traditional empiricism defined experience must be conceived as ancillary capacities discriminating qualitative detail within these units or wholes. Also, besides having this synoptic power, value experience must be conceived in depth. At least, in the mature individual it must be conceived as operating in terms of a store of concepts and presuppositions developed in the past and interpreting the present, illuminating the depths of the wholes in question. Finally, like all other forms of experience, it must be conceived as having a telic structure, as guided by aims and goals and ends, although these aims and goals and ends may be numerous, and many of them may be "unconscious" in the sense of not being explicitly known to the agent at the time he is acting on them.

Value experience so understood, while it is obviously very different from the simple-idea or simple-impression experience of traditional British empiricism, seems to include only the most elementary and indispensable factors needed for one to be aware of what he is in fact aware of in the value situation. In this sense, it contains what is essential for our purposes. No doubt, a treatise would be required to delineate in detail all the aspects of experience in the meaning here assigned it. But our aim now is to indicate merely the broad lines of experience that we shall assume are available to method in value theory.

As to its methodological role, experience is first of all the source of the "raw materials" of theory. It delivers to consciousness an awareness of the concrete layout and innumerable details of the value field, out of which the theoretic description of the principles of the field must be constructed. It also serves with some qualifications as a court of appeal for testing the features of the theoretic description. I say "with some qualifications" because value experience, being grounded on factors that are capable of error, such as the apprehending powers of sensation, intellect, and the like, the arsenal of interpretative concepts, and the telic components mentioned above, is not *prima facie* infallible, and in its first form often needs correction. However, we shall see[20] that it also has in it immanent principles of correction which can guide purgation of it in its *prima facie* form of disqualifying error, where this is needed.

The rationalist element in the methodology of value theory has at least a dual function. First, it is an effort to build consistency into the theoretical description, so that the many sides of this description fit together into a coherent whole. Second, it serves as a constant critic of the value experiences used as the basis and test of theory. Generally, its aim here is to determine the knowledge of details of the value field that this experience actually yields. This involves purifying the experience of misinterpretations, and indicating what

---

[20] Pp. 78-81 and next paragraph.

efforts toward self-correction if any are necessary in the telic principle of the experience for the genuine value disclosures of this experience to be clear. Thus, one might say that the role of reason in value theory is at once abstract and concrete. It seeks to achieve abstract conceptional unity in the theory, and it seeks to realize concrete clarity in the experiential value data or information about the polar variety and structure of the value situation. And only value experience whose data has been purged by rational reflection is properly the court of appeal for testing the features of the theoretical description.

To sum up, in the various areas of human life, a value situation is a transaction of subject and object governed by a telic structure. In innumerable instances, the subject as an experient is aware in some degree of the situation, either as a whole or in some of its unit details, and this awareness or cognition, however narrow or comprehensive, yields the *prima facie* data of value theory. But reason also is an essential of method, being needed to give an overall consistency to theory, and to purge the data of experience of any misinterpretation or error, including an indication of what may be needed, if anything, for the telic principle of the experience to meet the requirements of a satisfactory standard in the situation. These two roles of reason, abstract and concrete, are not to be understood as its sole functions in value knowledge or theory. But they are contributions reason can appropriately make to method here, and therefore are demands that the normative side of good procedure can properly make of reason in this cognitive undertaking.

Were we writing a treatise on method in value theory, we would have to recognize many detailed functions of reason: to construct definitions, to clarify assumptions, to develop arguments, and the like. But such topics are not germane to our present purpose. However, there is one point about the role of reason that probably should be mentioned. Sometimes it is said that the chief role of reason in method is postulation,[21] or setting up purely theoretical propositions, which are to be confirmed or disconfirmed by experience. This seems to us to introduce a kind of artificial separation between theory and experience, like the *a priori* and the empirical, so that their actual congruence can only seem unlikely or

[21] F. C. S. Northrop, *The Meeting of East and West* (New York: Macmillan Co., 1946), Chap. VIII, pp. 301-302, *passim.*

the work of a pre-established harmony. In any case, the proper *architect* of a value theory, we would suggest, is imagination, not reason, where imagination is understood as creative imagination, or, more specifically, as a power loaded with the details of experience yet moving always toward new over-all unities and novel syntheses of these details.[22] The role of reason in theory here is more one of purification and emendation, of introducing into an imaginative projection full internal coherence where this may be lacking. A value theory is not a foreign autonomous imposition from on high upon a heterogeneity of external data. It is making over-all complex sense of the data of our experience. It is working from within the data outward, as imagination does. Reason, it may be said, supplies the principle of logical order to imagination. But the more concrete and fact-cultured power of imagination itself works up the data of experience into inclusive internal order, furnishing thus in principle what good theory successfully developed is asked to supply. No doubt, if a value theory were capable of precise quantification, and, to gain maximum simplicity, it seemed desirable to replace its imaginative synthesis with an artificially rigorous system of mathematical variables specially invented for that purpose, reason would be the inventor and postulator of this independent theoretical construction. But in its present state value theory does not seem ripe for the introduction of such an artificial simplification and of a purely theoretical deductive order.

In the value field, then, a good theory must meet two tests, rational and empirical. It must be self-consistent or fit together into a unitary whole. Otherwise, its meaning is uncertain or indeterminate. This is the rational test. But it must also take into its account, or have a place within its account for, the data including the structural data of experience, as purged of cognitive limitations. It must fit the "facts" as these facts are known in critical experience. This is the empirical test. Insofar as a theory meets these tests, it is logically sound and factually solid. Hence, these would seem to be the major requirements of a good theory as theory, or as a theoretical construction.[23]

---

[22] Cf. D. W. Gotshalk, *Art and the Social Order* (Chicago: University of Chicago Press, 1947, 1951; New York: Dover Publications, Inc., 1962), Chap. III.

[23] D. W. Gotshalk, *Metaphysics in Modern Times* (Chicago: University of Chicago Press, 1940), pp. 10-12.

Obviously, these requirements of a theory are very high. That they are met in any given case must always be a matter for investigation. Hence, the theory of value we have stated and shall proceed to develop, and indeed the theory of value knowledge set forth in this chapter, are to be understood as hypotheses, not as finalities, as complex ideas to be appropriately tested further. The general aim of our discussion throughout this book on its methodological side will be to present as a hypothesis a theory of value and of value knowledge that meets or is able to meet the above two tests.

In this chapter, we have contended that value knowledge exists and is possible, that value statements make a cognitive claim and have a cognitive content, that this knowledge and cognitive content are to be found in experience and often obtained by direct insight into the situation being experienced, and that a good value theory is a complex idea developed by imagination from experience and able to meet the two tests appropriately placed upon it by reason and experience.

We shall describe now details of our value theory, keeping in mind the requirements of these two tests, and we shall discuss first the three foreground components of the value situation, beginning with the subject.

III

SUBJECT

Subjectivism

"Subjective" has several meanings. For some the "subjective" means whatever is different in experience for different people, the "objective" whatever is the common, the same for all. If a quality or the result of a laboratory test is the same for all of its qualified experients, it is said to be objective, and if not, subjective or subjectively tinged; and subjectivism is any doctrine that this or that—secondary qualities or beauty or value—is subjective and not objective in this sense. This version of "subjective" and "objective" states a useful distinction, and we shall avail ourselves of it later in a different connection. But, in our more general discussion, the "subjective" will mean whatever is part of the subject pole of the human value transaction even if this is common or the same for all; and subjectivism will be the claim that value resides exclusively or primarily in this subject pole. More specifically, in the discussion now to follow of recent subjectivists, who ordinarily think of the subject as an individual human being possessing "states of mind," subjectivism will be the claim that value resides exclusively or primarily in some "state of mind or consciousness" of individual human beings, such as pleasure, interest, or satisfaction.

Subjectivism in this sense covers a wide range of recent value theory. Obviously, it includes the positivists and the extreme emotivists, Carnap, Reichenbach, Russell, Ayer. Equally included are those who equate "good" with an attitude of favor or approval, a pro attitude, with or without additional subjective factors such as an urge to command or persuade, for example, Stevenson, Nowell-Smith, McGreal.[1] But the range of subjectivism, as just defined, is much broader. It includes the recent varieties of hedonism. Schlick writes: "Thus there remains no alternative to locating the characteristic of value once more in an immediate datum. . . . Our own criterion is of this sort: the corresponding experience is simply the feeling of pleasure. . . . According to our opinion the *essence* of value is completely exhausted by it."[2] Hilliard writes: "Value is affectivity," and "the sole *value*, positive affectivity," where "affectivity (or hedonic tone) is a class of which the sole members are pleasantness [positive affectivity], indifference, and unpleasantness."[3] Also coming under subjectivism in the present sense would be theories describing value as satisfaction. Parker writes: "values belong wholly to the inner world, to the world of mind"; "we must look for value not in the things themselves, but in the desires and satisfactions which they promote." "The satisfaction of desire is the real value."[4] Perry's interest theory claims to be a relational view, but it defines interest as an "all-pervasive characteristic of the motor-affective life, this *state, act, attitude,* or *disposition of favor or disfavor,*" and conceives interest "to be the original source and constant feature of all value" and things as deriving or acquiring value from it: "Any object, whatever it be, acquires value when any interest, whatever it be, is taken in it."[5] That is, according to Perry, value originally and fundamentally lies in interest, and whatever value objects have is conferred upon them by this subjective factor. C. I. Lewis holds

---

[1] Ian McGreal, "A Naturalistic Analysis of Value Terms," *Philosophy and Phenomenological Research,* Vol. X, No. 1 (Sept., 1949), pp. 73-84.

[2] Moritz Schlick, *Problems of Ethics* (New York: Prentice-Hall, Inc., 1939), p. 105. Italics in text.

[3] A. L. Hilliard, *The Forms of Value* (New York: Columbia University Press, 1950), pp. 42, 205, 14.

[4] DeWitt H. Parker, *Human Values* (New York: Harper & Bros., 1931), pp. 20, 19, 20. Cf. Henry D. Aiken, "Reflections on Dewey's Questions About Value" in *Value: A Cooperative Inquiry,* ed. by Ray Lepley (New York: Columbia University Press, 1949), pp. 23-24.

[5] R. B. Perry, *General Theory of Value* (Cambridge: Harvard University Press, 1926), pp. 115-116. Italics in text.

a parallel theory, but places the fundamental form of value in intrinsic value defined as immediately found value. He adds: *"no objective existent has strictly intrinsic value; all values in objects are extrinsic only,"* and later remarks: "Thus the conception is that the only thing intrinsically valuable—valuable for its own sake— is a goodness immediately found or findable and unmistakable when disclosed: all values of any sort, including all values attributable to objects, are extrinsic, and valued for the sake of their possible contribution to such realizations of the immediately good."[6] Finally, Rice tries to combine affective and conative factors in the meaning of value, affectivity or agreeableness constituting the identifying property of value, and interest or conation its matrix meaning.[7]

In a critical volume on current value theory, each of these examples of subjectivism would deserve separate detailed discussion. Here only one or two comments on aspects of a few of them can be made, along with a general criticism of the doctrine as a whole.

To say "X is good" means that you have a pleasant emotion toward X, specifically an emotion or attitude of approval or favor, a pro attitude seems generally correct, although we do sometimes say "X is good" where X is a rival, a clever lawyer, or other person or thing or activity of which we do not approve at all, even heartily detest. However, where the assertion "X is good" does mean that we favor, approve, and the like, we ordinarily do not mean that our approval or favoring or prizing makes X good, but, more often, that our approval or the like is a recognition that X is good, and that we approve or favor or prize X because we recognize its goodness. Indeed, in eating, traveling, appreciating a new painting, or reading a book of philosophy, a favoring attitude often arises only after we have finished and found out what is good in the activity or object. The emotion follows after discovering the value and hence cannot create or constitute the value, since the value was found before the emotion was felt. Similar remarks apply to an interest theory such as Perry's. That we have an interest in

---

[6] C. I. Lewis, *An Analysis of Knowledge and Valuation* (La Salle, Ill.: Open Court Publishing Co., 1946), pp. 387, 397. Italics in text. Cf. E. F. Carrett, *Ethical and Political Thinking* (Oxford: Clarendon Press, 1947), p. 99.

[7] Philip B. Rice, *On the Knowledge of Good and Evil* (New York: Random House, Inc., 1955), pp. 208 ff., 101 ff., *passim*.

anything may in general be regarded as a sign that it has a *prima facie* value for us. But often it is something in the thing itself that aroused our interest, and we became interested because we saw that the thing had a value for us. Indeed, all that interest surely confers on an object is an interest in it, and whether the object is really to our interest depends on factors additional to the favor or interest we show.

Hedonism, of which the general positions of Schlick and Hilliard are instances, has been subjected to lengthy criticism that is generally well known, and we need emphasize only a point or two in the charges that still seem to hold against it. Thus, it is difficult to see how mere pleasure can be regarded as the prime or sole good if we regard the pleasure of a sadist, a kleptomaniac, or a dedicated murderer as not good. To determine the good, some sorting principle additional to pleasure, to select between pleasures, would seem to be required. Nor does it seem correct in many instances to say that I perform an act (psychological hedonism) or should perform it (ethical hedonism) for pleasure; for example, drink a glass of milk. I may do it for pleasure, but also for nourishment, refreshment, or companionship; and all of these values and others, each of which is analytically distinct from pleasure and each other, may be part of the value of the act, and any one of them may be the explicit reason why I did so act, or should so have acted. In these instances pleasure seems too thin or narrow a characterization of the good, while in the instances cited at the beginning of this paragraph it seems too broad a characterization. The satisfaction theory of Parker, the immediate realization theory of Lewis, I believe, are open to criticisms similar to those of hedonism. Of any satisfaction or immediate realization, a drunken driver's or a dope addict's, we may ask whether it is good, and be quite unconvinced by the fact that the person in question finds or thinks he finds it good. Also, Lewis' life-long continuum or gestalt of satisfactions or immediate realizations may describe well the intrinsic side of the good life of a flourishing mole, unless the continuum as a whole must be an immediate satisfaction to be intrinsically good, in which case it does not seem to describe the intrinsic side of the good life of any being. But, in any case, it does not explicitly entail any specific human content or give a very rounded picture of a good life in specifically human terms.

These criticisms of several varieties of subjectivism may be supplemented by two criticisms that apply to the doctrine as a whole.

First, as we have said, subjectivism claims that value resides exclusively or primarily in some conscious psychological state of the subject, for example, pleasure, satisfaction, immediate realization. The value of objects is secondary and derivative, conferred on them because they cause such states or are objects of some psychological attitude such as favor, approval, interest. Even with human values, and abstracting from all others, such as the value of flowers to bees, worms to the soil, soil to a crop, and more, this view of the value of objects does not seem to be correct. For example, a food is commonly recognized to have nutritional value if it meets certain requirements, for example, has certain vitamins and other biochemical components. And this recognition may be independent of whether any individual psychological agent whatsoever favors, approves, or has a conscious interest in eating the food, and of whether the food has given or will give pleasure, satisfaction, or any immediate realization whatsoever. Moreover, a person may consume the food not knowing it is nutritious, and not enjoy it at all. Yet the food may have nutritional value. Indeed, in numerous cases such as intravenous feeding of patients in coma this value exists and operates in full force without the subject having any conscious state, pleasure, satisfaction, or immediate realization, or taking any interest at all in the food.

In general, as we have already suggested and will argue later, objects belong to domains of their own, and each domain has a purpose structure of its own independent of the individual psychology of diverse human agents, and if objects meet the requirements of this purpose structure, or insofar as they do, they will have value there, whether or not they arouse approval or pleasure or any other conscious state in any interested set of human agents.

Second, subjectivism generally misconstrues the nature of subjective value itself. It conceives this value primarily as a psychological datum, affective or conative, taken in itself: pleasure, satisfaction, striving, immediate realization; whereas it is commonly and more accurately conceived to be such a datum which meets certain specifications. A pleasure that is a distraction from serious activity requiring our immediate attention is commonly regarded not as a good but a nuisance, or worse. A satisfaction in poor work is not commonly thought to be a good but a failing, even if or especially if the satisfaction is intense or large. Were the naturalistic fallacy merely the identifying of good with a given natural psychological fact or datum instead of the very confused and complicated affair that a study of G. E. Moore, its foster father, has led some to believe,[8] one might say that the subjectivist here is guilty of the naturalistic fallacy. He takes a natural datum as the good, and ignores that which alone might induce one to consider such a datum good—its normative adequacy, or its satisfying certain requirements.

The subjectivist may reply that this criticism misses his point. His view is that pleasure in itself, and satisfaction in itself, taken intrinsically, are good, and indeed the good, and are never bad. They are always immediately and unreservedly accepted and preferred to their opposites. Of course, he may agree, in common life they get mixed up with various activities and things, and come to draw to themselves some of the bad odor of some of these activities and things. But in themselves or intrinsically they are always good, and that much good in any situation, however bad, which involves them.

This reply, however, does not altogether remove the difficulty. Not only in common life but elsewhere including the life of the subjectivist, pleasure, satisfaction, immediate realization exist as pleasure *of*, satisfaction *in*, realization *of*. As subjective states, they never exist in themselves, but determinately—for example, the pleasure *of* sunshine, laziness, and so on. To discuss these states realistically and concretely they must be considered as determinate, in which case their subjective value quality in some instances leaves much to be desired. Moreover, even if, unlike the good Berkeley, we could catch pleasure in itself, satisfaction in itself, and the like, and experience them in isolation and in this sense intrinsically, the subjectivist's interpretation of subjective value would not be established. For while we might immediately accept these states in all such cases and prefer them to their opposites, it would be only because they measured up immediately and in a superior way to certain demands of the organism, or met certain

---

[8] Cf. William K. Frankena, "The Naturalistic Fallacy," *Mind,* Vol. 48 (1939), pp. 464-477.

specifications. If pleasure in itself, for example, did not instantly meet certain specifications and not others, it would not be accepted immediately, or at all. The organism with its inherently normative bent devaluates at once, or over time, if it has time, whatever states do not meet its demands, as we shall see. Thus, it is not these states as such that constitute subjective value, as the subjectivist believes, but these states, if any, as satisfying immediately and in a superior way certain inherent requirements of the human being.

Whatever its faults, it is only fair to add, subjectivism in value theory has considerable undeniable merits. If it seems to exaggerate the status of subjective good and to misconstrue its nature, it has brought to attention with sharpest emphasis a great array of the most precious personal values. Also, unlike objectivism which tends to conceive values as independent of the individual, and hints at a superindividual and even superhuman origin and authority for value, it has underlined the basically human and individual side of human value. In recent value theory particularly, subjectivism has flourished vigorously in Great Britain and America, where the traditional individualistic orientation to culture has made it strongly harmonious with the social environment. Undoubtedly, subjectivism has also been given added impetus by our Western technological civilization, wherein people are conditioned to believe that everything outside the subject, often including other subjects, is or should be an instrument of subjective pleasure and power. However this may be, and even if subjectivism seems wrong as a complete doctrine and mistaken about the principle of its own area, it does require us to recognize that this area has a principle and a relative independence of its own, demanding study in its own right.

We now proceed to a few of the details of such a study, and first to some general considerations about human nature.

Orientation

The human being, it seems descriptively correct to say, is value oriented. From his first breath to his last conscious moments he is a center of directional striving appeased only by some good, or the promise of a good. The primacy of practical reason seems better described as the primacy of goal-seeking. This property has been asserted of all organisms. "Among the many things that are characteristic of organisms is that they strive toward goals."[9] However characteristic it may be of organisms of all types, the property of goal-seeking seems basic, spontaneous, and original in the make-up of the human type.

"Of normativeness or goal seeking," Rice writes, "This principle is genuinely a principle: it formulates a basic structural presupposition of our actions."[10] "It is inherent in the frame of reference of 'action,'" says Parsons, "that it is 'normatively oriented.'"[11] And Boring: "There is really no such thing as unmotivated behavior."[12] Regarding this normativeness, Rice continues:

We espouse it, then, we may say, because we are men, and man is by nature a normative animal. This is in some sense a *fact*, a fundamental datum. All living beings are loaded and cocked when they come into existence. We can put the matter either metaphysically by saying that the Platonic Eros is of their essence, or scientifically by saying that the goal-seeking urge is thrust upon them by their metabolism, life being a generation of energy that must be expended. It is of their nature that men—not to mention children—are trying to go somewhere. Their perplexities arise, not from the need to justify the fundamental restlessness or vectorial character of existence. . . . The problem is not how normativeness gets into the make-up of the human or sub-human animal, but how to channel it. . . .[13]

This original goal-seeking urge of human nature has been given many names, from the Platonic Eros mentioned by Rice to the Freudian libido, and along the way the instinct of self-preservation and the will to power. Today probably the most widely used name in general psychology for it is drive. All such terms emphasize some important aspects of the goal-seeking urge, but are also linked with theories and associations that place certain undesirable limitations on it. To avoid these limitations and associations we have used a different term, the Greek *telos*, and we shall try to

---

[9] Robert B. MacLeod, "Teleology and Theory of Human Behaviour," *Science*, Vol. 125, No. 3246 (March 15, 1957), p. 479.

[10] Rice, *On the Knowledge of Good and Evil*, p. 178.

[11] Max Weber, *The Theory of Social and Economic Organization*, Introduction by Talcott Parsons, ed. (New York: Oxford University Press, 1947), p. 12.

[12] Edwin G. Boring, "Psychology" in *What Is Science?*, ed. by James Newman (New York: Simon and Schuster Co., 1955), p. 310; cf. Abraham A. Maslow (ed.), *New Knowledge in Human Values* (New York: Harper & Bros., 1959), pp. 120-126; Gordon W. Allport, *Personality* (New York: Henry Holt & Co., 1937), Chaps. X-XV, especially pp. 319 ff.

[13] Rice, *On the Knowledge of Good and Evil*, pp. 178-179. Italics in text.

develop our own specific interpretation of the goal-seeking urge around this term, which represents here what we have called elsewhere the principle of self-determinacy.[14]

One property of this goal-seeking urge, as we shall interpret it, deserves immediate emphasis. This is its basically relational character. This normative striving is a reaching out toward objects, and in the first instance, among other things, toward objects physically external to the subject—for example, mother's breast. The human being is object oriented. He is an incomplete creature, almost always with needs of some sort requiring fulfillment. You might describe his goal-seeking property as a reaching out toward wholeness. In any case, it is a reaching out toward objects and directed toward the values in objects. Hence, the necessity that objects be conceived as antecedently having values, and to some extent as precompetent to meet telic requirements. Without such competency human life long ago would have congealed and perished.

Still, while the *telos* is a reaching out toward objects and directed toward the values in objects, it is also a reaching out for self-enhancement, for a "building up" of the subject. There is no paradox here. The *telos* is a relational principle and so of necessity involves at least two "terms." The aim is initially toward objects, but, as relationally involving the subject in striving, it is intent also on an achievement by the subject. Even in the most self-effacing act, and I mean *self*-effacing, the aim is for an objective good that also achieves the subjective fulfillment of self-effacement. This does not mean, for example, that an altruistic act is necessarily or usually egoistic in the sense of being aimed primarily at some subjective good. It is usually aimed primarily at an objective good. But the very fulfillment of this aim is a subjective achievement and has a *prima facie* value in the being of the subject.

As a first approximation, we might say, a subjective value occurs when an activity, attitude, state of being, or other possession of a subject meets certain requirements of the *telos* in its engagement with objects. The value consists in the adequacy of the possession to the requirements, or the fulfillment of the requirements, but it is mediated by the relation between the possession and the requirements. In its engagement with objects which are so various in

---

[14] D. W. Gotshalk, *Structure and Reality* (New York: Dial Press, 1937), Chaps. I, VI.

their value properties, the *telos* itself takes innumerable directions, and, as a result, there is a vast panoply of activities, states, attitudes, and the like, having subjective value. Even when these are described in general terms, they compose a lengthy list. Depending on the subjective and objective circumstances, and the aim, this list includes certain kinds of pleasure but also certain kinds of pain, for example, the pain of suspense, of hard work, and the like, certain kinds of satisfaction but also certain kinds of dissatisfaction, for example, discontent with a poor performance, and so forth. There are, however, so many more of these activities, states, attitudes that a detailed enumeration would be encyclopedic: health, work, freedom, power, talent, poise, efficiency, self-restraint, survival, growth, creativeness, friendliness, love, courage, self-respect, morale, impartiality. This list is a small selection only from what are conventionally considered "subjective" goods and it might have included many other activities, states, attitudes not conventionally so considered: indifference, anger, black looks, *ad infinitum*.

This last statement calls attention to a point already noted in the discussion of hedonism and elsewhere: namely, it is not the psychological state, activity, attitude, as such, that is the value. The value lies in the state, activity, or attitude satisfying certain demands. Also, the proper demands may so vary that in a certain situation black looks, rather than friendliness, may be more nearly the valuable and appropriate attitude. It has commonly been noted that no "virtue" is all "virtue," that a good heart may even lead to one's undoing. This ambivalence of "virtue" or "excellence" is due to conceiving it abstractly, as a general state or activity, intrinsically complete, rather than relationally. When this last is done, and the subjective good is seen to be only whatever state or activity or attitude meets certain demands, or more precisely, the meeting of these demands, the so-called ambivalence of "virtue" or "excellence" disappears, as does the possibility of any neat and finite list of the states, attitudes, and activities having subjective values.

Nevertheless, subjective values do fall into certain broad types, and it will help greatly toward the clarification of the area of subjective values to distinguish and discuss some of these types.

Types

Of these types, the first is intrinsic value and its contrast, extrinsic value. Subjectivists generally have construed this distinction as the same as between subjective and objective. As we have said, the final good, the good in itself, or genuine good, they hold is a subjective state: pleasure, satisfaction, immediate realization, while the value of objects—insofar as they may be said to have value— is as means or external causes of valuable subjective states. However, subjectivists are not alone in finding intrinsic values solely in subjective states. G. E. Moore, for example, who is commonly regarded as an objectivist in value theory, holds that there are only two intrinsic goods, personal affection and aesthetic enjoyment.[15] Both of these would commonly be called subjective states. Generally, however, it has been the subjectivists who have developed the view identifying the intrinsic and the subjective, the extrinsic and the objective.

A dispute with subjectivists here need not be merely terminological, that is, over a preference in word usage. The question may also be whether the use of terms in a given way reveals or conceals certain important distinctions. In the next chapter, we shall argue that a useful meaning can be assigned to the phrase "intrinsic objective value." An equally useful meaning we shall now argue can be given the phrase "extrinsic subjective value." If this is the case, the restrictions placed by the subjectivist on "intrinsic" and "extrinsic" seem unwarranted.

A subject's activities and states, let us grant at the outset, may have intrinsic value. To feel a certain way, for example, in excellent health, may not merely help you to work better or help you to raise the value quality of a certain group undertaking. But it may be valuable on its own intrinsic merits, as a state which meets the appropriate requirements of good in its own right. Obviously, however, this does not prohibit such a state from having the additional values just noted—namely, helping you to work better or to raise the value quality of a group undertaking. In this sense, the subjective state, intrinsically worthy, has extrinsic value, and this value, as attaching to a subject's state, may properly be called "subjective extrinsic value."

Of all recent writers on value theory, John Dewey has probably emphasized most, under the term "instrumental," the extrinsic type of value. Indeed, in his zeal for the instrumental and his distrust of dualisms, Dewey sometimes has seemed to fuse intrinsic values

---

[15] G. E. Moore, *Principia Ethica* (Cambridge: Cambridge University Press, 1903, 1954), Chap. VI. See also below, pp. 52-54.

with their extrinsic outcomes.[16] Now, it is true that the intrinsic values of certain subjective states may not be self-evident, and may even have to be learned. Further, it may be true that every subjective state is connected with antecedents and consequences, and so is part of a means-end continuum. Still, a subjective state in a subject-object transaction has its own concrete character and accordingly may itself uniquely meet certain requirements. In this sense, intrinsic subjective values are always possible, and are distinct, and are as real as instrumental values and not to be confused with their extrinsic outcomes.

Perhaps, in this connection, a further distinction should be introduced. Often intrinsic values are called "final" values, and in one sense, such usage seems justified. The intrinsic value of an item may be said to be a kind of final or terminal property constitutive of its decisive being when the item is in being. Still, it may be more suitable to reserve the term "final" value for the sum of an item's intrinsic and extrinsic values. This total value is the value of a subjective state, activity, attitude in its full spread, in its "finished" or final form, and only when we see a subjective item in its intrinsic and extrinsic stature do we see it with finality, or in terms of all of the ends (*fini*) it effectively serves. In this sense, the final value of a subjective item is not merely what it is at the moment of its being, but what it amounts to in the life of the subject, and of all other subjects actually involved extrinsically.

Besides intrinsic and extrinsic values, another classification applicable to subjective value is enjoyment and achievement value. Enjoyment and achievement values are customarily correlated respectively with the affective (feeling) and conative (will) aspects of human nature. To be faithful to the triangle of capacities in traditional psychology we should also include here the cognitive (reason) aspect of human nature, and knowledge and cognitive value. But knowledge has already been discussed in one respect, and shall be discussed later in other respects, and enjoyment and achievement values have certain claims for independent consideration. Two points, however, might be appropriately made about knowledge in passing, both illustrative.

First, knowledge illustrates the interpenetration of the three

---

[16] Cf. John Dewey, "Theory of Valuation," *International Encyclopedia of Unified Science,* Vol. II, No. 4 (Chicago: University of Chicago Press, 1939), Sec. vi, *passim.*

values here in question. For the gaining of real knowledge is an achievement, and knowledge itself, as well as the gaining of it, may be enjoyed both for what it is and for what it might or does produce. That is, achievement and enjoyment value may interpenetrate cognitive value, knowledge, or truth. Second, knowledge also illustrates very vividly the theory of value we are developing throughout this analysis. Not any statement or form of words, nor any array of symbols, is knowledge. Only statements or other symbolic structures that meet certain requirements are knowledge. The particular requirements for knowledge are the special concern of the logician and epistemologist, and are exemplified in science and certain activities of everyday life. They need not concern us now. The chief point is that symbolic structures must meet certain standards or fulfill certain demands to have cognitive value, or be knowledge. Not any set of symbols existing as a psychological fact or datum is by this fact alone in possession of truth value.

Turning now to enjoyment and achievement values, we may note first their deep-seated character. They are correlated not only with psychological aspects of the human being but also with physical and biological aspects. As physical, the human being is an open energy system or a system open to the environment, and he is continually absorbing and expending energy in accordance with the laws of energy within this environment. Moreover, as an organism with biological needs, these absorptions and expenditures of energy take specific directions in efforts to meet these needs, and in the successful surviving organism these absorptions and expenditures presumably result in primitive satisfactions as well as primitive accomplishments. Thus, enjoyment and achievement are not rarefied "mentalistic" phenomena. Based on the total physical and biological layout of the human subject, achievements may reach into all levels of the subject's being, while enjoyments may occur at the dimmest level of consciousness.

This is not to claim that these subjective human values can be derived from some subhuman physical or biologic fact in nature. It is rather to suggest, as I have said, that these values have great depth in human nature. Also, it is to suggest that the range of these values, so primitively based, may be very wide. Indeed, enjoyment value may include the pleasure we take in anything: breathing and eating, but no less, a reverie, an adventure, the sunset, our country. The value is in the pleasure or other subjective state as meeting certain specifications, but provided it meets these, the subjective state having value may be focused on any sort of object. Of course, a requirement of certain subjective values may be that the subject be focused on a certain type of object. For example, a requirement of aesthetic enjoyment value is that the pleasure be in the aesthetic aspects of an object, and if in contemplating a work of art a stray practical or scientific thought passes through the mind and gives pleasure, there may be enjoyment and even value, but in this instance not aesthetic enjoyment and value. The chief point, however, is that enjoyment value, while subjective or the value of a subjective state, is not limited in its scope to the inner resources of the subject. These inner resources—thoughts, images, and the like—may furnish many occasions for enjoyment, or none at all. But the whole wide world of "external" objects and actions is open also, and capable within limits of being the source of such enjoyments.

Enjoyments as affective states are sometimes described as passive, and insofar as they are changes which are undergone in submission to objects, enjoyments clearly are. But in actual life even the most passive enjoyments involve some effort. A gratuity from nature— bright sunshine on a cold day—to be enjoyed requires at least that one open up one's being to it, and give it some attention. The kinds of active effort and achievement involved in enjoyment will vary. As good an example as any is play or recreation, for example, games. Here an end is set up, usually the attaining of a superior score within stipulated rules; and in games between able opponents, gaining this end may involve the expenditure of considerable skill and effort. Indeed, achievement values may enliven play throughout and not be negligible. But in play proper or recreation, the superior achievement of this end is mainly a means, and apart from incidental ego satisfaction, the substantive values are in the pleasures of exercise with its often healthful consequences, and usually for adults, the pleasures of diversion, the forgetting or putting to one side temporarily of the more "serious" and far-reaching problems of the workaday world. To be sure, in professional sport, where "play" becomes "work," this order is inverted. The achievement of victory, usually yielding superior monetary rewards, is really the end, while the enjoyment of exercise and diversion, at least for the players, becomes incidental. In pure play, however, enjoyment is the main end, and winning incidental. But, even in pure play, achievement in the sense of attaining victory or a good score may have value, as adding incentive and zest to the exercise and diversion, and yielding immediate ego satisfaction. Enjoyment, however, may occur in some measure for some people even in unskilled and poor-scoring play. But it is more likely to occur for most people when achievement of a higher order inter-penetrates enjoyment and serves to give it added qualities.

Achievement suggests the "work" side of life, as enjoyment the "play" side, the active against the passive, the doer against the playboy. And as enjoyment often consists of pleasure had in sub-mission to objects, so achievement often consists of attaining goals by active dominance and mastery of media leading to these goals. In much achievement, enjoyment is not a conspicuous component. Tension, suspense, delay, uncertainty, patience, forbearance, sweat-ing effort, all the more trying states of mind, useful but not titillat-ing, tend to crowd the center of activity. Of course, one may enjoy the struggle and delight in the outcome. But the achievement is the struggle attaining its aim, and the affective accompaniment is a variable depending on the kind of struggle, the kind of aim, the kind of subject and circumstances, and the kind of outcome.

Why achieve, or even try, if there is no fun in it? A sufficient answer might be that there is more to life than fun, as there is more to human nature than its affective component. But two points should be added to what was said in the preceding paragraph.

First, while enjoyment may not be conspicuous in much achieve-ment, this does not mean that it is totally absent. One may do something; an artist deathly ill may work at a composition, because he believes he "has to," regardless of the physical or psychological obstacles standing in the way. He may create in considerable dis-comfort. Yet even here, as the work proceeds and he succeeds, a dim or grim pleasure may invade the activity, each tiny success as it builds toward the accomplished work registering a moment of relief or excitement in his consciousness. No successful achievement is likely to be altogether without at least such muffled undertones of enjoyment. Nor need unsuccessful efforts at certain points en-tirely lack them, although, under very trying circumstances, both successful and unsuccessful achievements may as a matter of fact not have them.

Second, while enjoyment may not be conspicuous in some cases, and virtually absent in very extreme cases, it provides one of the best stimuli to high achievement and thereby becomes included in some of the most strenuous accomplishments. It is true, for example, that one may "hate one's work" yet do it well. But with most people, as Aristotle said long ago, pleasure adds to the accuracy and efficiency of an activity. Indeed, according to general belief, ideally desirable work is serviceable work with an element of fun in it, or good paying work that one would do or like to do even if one did not get paid for it. In any case, with most people enjoyment appears to add to the zest and sureness of work, as achievement often adds to the zest and quality of play. And while one would be foolhardy always to insist upon or expect high enjoyment in achievements of the most demanding type, including moral and social achievements no less than artistic and scientific ones, they need not be without deep-lying agreeableness, and even moments of gaiety.

As with enjoyments so with achievements, the range of their values is very wide. These values may be found in any domain of human activity and in the creation of any entities of objective value, from physical structures such as roads and bridges to political institutions and works of art and science. Nor are achievement values confined to activities in "public" life. They may enter into the most secret workings of the heart. Building an inner attitude for dealing successfully with a particular personal problem may seem a very slight achievement *sub specie aeternitatis*, but it may have precious values for the person who does it. Achievements in this "innermost" subjective region extend from a momentary inner front against danger to the most long-range attitude crystallizing a whole philosophy of life. Self-mastery, control of impulse and feeling, all of the personal virtues, courage, honesty, and the like, illustrate the variety of this inner achievement at its best. Of all of these subjective items, certainly one of the most significant shaped by achievement activity is the personality of the subject.

Before discussing this, one point about achievements and enjoyments should be further emphasized. Achievements just because they are achievements, enjoyments just because they are enjoyments, are not values. Nor do they have value. Like other psychological activities and states they have value if and only if they meet a certain standard or conform to certain requirements. The enjoyment of envy and spite, the achievement of large scale destruction à la Hitler, are as real as the enjoyment of mental peace, or the achievement of international decency. Also, in their curious way they embody the orientation and personality of the human beings exhibiting them, and like the so-called "death instinct," they are cherished by some as if they were good or pathways to good. But of such things we certainly raise the question of whether they *are* good or pathways to good, that is, whether they meet the requirements of value. Only enjoyments and achievements doing this, or in the degree that they do this, have value, and were intended in the preceding discussion as illustrative of enjoyment and achievement values.

Personality

Subjective values not only constitute general types such as intrinsic and extrinsic, and cognitive, achievement, and enjoyment values. They also enter into a particular subject's life and form an individuated pattern in his being. In doing this, they signalize the distinctive telic bent of his nature, or what might be called the core of his personality.

As commonly understood, personality is made up of inherited and acquired factors. The inherited factors are typified by "temperament," which is often taken as the salient component of a personality, as when one speaks of an individual having a mild or a volatile personality. The acquired factors are typified by "character," in a broad sense the "moral character" of the individual, his settled disposition toward certain types of acts, developed by habit and practice. Sometimes "character" is taken as the leading component of personality, as when people speak of an individual as having an ill-developed or well-developed personality. The two components, inherited and acquired, are difficult to separate, and for our purposes do not need to be separated. The important point is to understand personality in its core as a complex telic fabric underlying the subjective value patterns as well as manifesting itself in action in terms of a scale of values. I say "personality in its core" because its telic fabric is embodied in a physical structure that may lend accent and luster to it, and personality in its fullest meaning probably should include this physical presence as well as the dynamic trait system it manifests.

This telic fabric, we have said, rests upon certain inherited factors, but it is also an outcome of growth. Talent, temperament, inborn needs and appetites, seem to hindsight innate in the creature, and, as experience proceeds, the personality seems to blossom from them. But this blossoming also appears to follow the directions indicated by the strongest external pressures and influences, so much so that some would explain all of the self as a social product or a product of the physical and social environment. The truth here, as elsewhere, seems to lie somewhere between extreme views. The physical and social environment is a formative power of the first magnitude. It furnishes the primary stimuli and the major opportunities. It arouses and limits the individual's being at every turn. But something more than stimuli and opportunities are needed for personality to become actual. Responses must be made, opportunities must be seized, and, above all, acts must be executed in ways possible to the individual. Only that can be accomplished by the individual which his resident nature and strivings can manage, even if it must be done only in some way that circumstances allow. The result is that the resident nature and strivings of the individual are transformed but also asserted, and it is this complex developed telic fabric, colored by temperament *and* social circumstances, that in its full spread constitutes the core of the individual's personality.[17]

In its being, personality is no simpler than in its genetic elements. Indeed, here it is more like a family of telic traits with multitudinous variables. We sometimes sum up a personality in a single word: dynamic, receptive, indecisive, self-sufficient, timid, carefree, indulgent, sympathetic, or whatever. Such descriptions seem appropriate and useful up to a point, since the center of personality tends to be a distinctive bent and so seems suitably set off by a differentiating term. But a so-called dynamic person in certain situations may be receptive, indecisive, self-sufficient, timid, carefree, indulgent, sympathetic, or whatever, although on the whole the best term for him may be dynamic. Or, he may be dynamic only when given certain opportunities, for example, appointed leader, and under other conditions, his dynamism may not be prominent. In short, personality in its nature would seem to be best described as an extensive profile of telic traits, the contours of which are

---

[17] Cf. D. W. Gotshalk, *Art and the Social Order* (Chicago: University of Chicago Press, 1947, 1951; New York: Dover Publications, Inc., 1962), Chap. III, sec. 5.

sometimes very sharp, sometimes very dim, depending on the individual and circumstances.

Several further observations seem needed to fill in the main outlines of our view.

First, while personality has definite genetic components and manifests definite qualities, it is obviously not understood by us as a fixed essence incapable of change. In a certain sense, some element or elements of a personality may be fixed and inflexible. A dominantly phlegmatic person may be momentarily jolted out of his characteristic attitude or mode of action by an extreme crisis. But he may soon revert to the *status quo ante*, and continue so indefinitely. In some people, however, a large number of traits often alter radically, even disappear for an extended time or permanently. These changes may take various forms. A strong trait of childhood may vanish apparently, only to return at a much later date and become tyrannical as age advances. Or, a deeply creative vein in a person may be sidetracked for years by other claims, then be recovered in a sudden change and become the dominant trait of the person. The growth of a virtue may lead to the concomitant growth of a vice, as when a person becoming more confident and incisive in his thought may also become more overbearing and insufferable in his manner. Or an individual may shed a whole constellation of traits and seem to become a quite different person, as when a grim or dour individual falls in love and becomes more "human," or an overly optimistic person becomes increasingly disillusioned.

But perhaps the most instructive type of personality change is not such as these, which may be largely unconscious or unpremeditated, but changes consciously undertaken. An individual with what he regards as a personality defect may set out deliberately to overcome it. He may be timid, overassertive, intemperate, self-centered, impulsive, prodigal, or egotistic. But by discipline and practice, despite repeated failures, he may erase the undesired trait from his personality. A whole library of trash has been published on how to improve one's personality, and, although many of the assumptions of such writing usually are naïve, particularly in regard to what improvement is and why the recommended improvements are desirable, the basic assumption that personality can be consciously changed in certain respects seems sound enough. One of the attractive characteristics of youth, as well as one of its exasperations, is the lack of sharp definition, or just the plain lack, of many traits of personality. This characteristic usually becomes more attractive and less exasperating when one sees what age does to youth's personality in so many cases. An alteration occurs, occasionally a vast improvement. But in too many instances the once seemingly infinite unfilled-in promise of youth gives way to an array of commonplace or conventional attitudes. Not merely details but the whole aspect of personality is grimly altered, often by effort.

Second, personalities vary not only over time but markedly among themselves at any given time. The variety here of course is enormous. The traits that may compose a personality form a very long list, of which those mentioned in the last few paragraphs, such as receptiveness, indecisiveness, self-sufficiency, timidity, carefreeness, self-indulgence, sympathy, overassertiveness, intemperance, self-centeredness, impulsiveness, prodigality, egotism, are only a small sample. A personality is usually composed of some large group of such traits, and in it, as compared with another, not only may the included traits be different (many personality traits being opposites often exclude each other), but the traits that are included may appear in any one of an indefinitely large number of degrees and proportions. Curiosity may be a microscopic trait in one person, an all-consuming "passion" in another. So may modesty or ruthlessness. By some kind of "chemistry" that we need not investigate, human beings actualize the possibilities of this wide variety so as to come up with personalities that have as much diversity (and sameness) as fingerprints or facial contours. A personality is really an individual way in which a galaxy of telic traits that are widely shared, and in some cases, such as curiosity, perhaps universally shared, appears in various degrees and combinations. And not only do the individual patterns differ in their inclusions and governing proportions, but in most cases the constituent traits, dominant or subordinate, are like "friendliness" or "curiosity," which name not a particular fixed trait but a whole gamut of closely related tendencies or proclivities.

The great variety of personalities and of the components of personality, however, does not make useless the analysis of personality by means of certain ideal types, for example, Dionysian and Apollonian, productive and nonproductive, libertarian and Puritan, inner-directed and outer-directed. If individuals in their full concrete nature *are* individuals, groups of individuals may still be alike in certain characteristics and tendencies—color of eyes and skin, and, no less, contour of personality. The delineation of ideal types in ethics and social studies may therefore shed much light on groups of individuals. Nor in connection with our own purpose does the great variety of personalities and of their components mean that a value appraisal—what is good and bad in personality—is not possible, since telic traits singly and in combination have determinate natures, and therefore under circumstances allowing their effective manifestation should be amenable to appraisal. But one point seems plain enough from the discussion in this section. "Personality" for us is not a value term. It is like enjoyment and achievement: its value comes in all sizes and shapes. This value is not given in its general nature but in its particular forms as meeting certain specifications. Sometimes, "personality" is used in a eulogistic sense, as when one says: "he is quite a personality!" But, in the sense we have used the term, everyone is or has a personality, the saint but no less the degenerate.

There remains, therefore, a question raised in the discussion of enjoyments and achievements and previously: the problem of the appraising standard, the determiner of the specifications. Our theory is that this standard is a relational principle, and the value of items is a relational property, the property of meeting the requirements of the principle. The discussion of the problem of the appraising standard will naturally come up in a consideration of the relational component of the value situation.

Meanwhile, the field of objective values calls for survey and clarification, and, as this will also raise certain problems regarding appraising standards, we shall proceed first to it.

IV

OBJECT

Objectivism

"Objective" as well as "subjective" is an ambiguous term. "Objective" may mean "independent of the whims, emotions, wishes, inclinations of an individual," as "subjective" may mean "dependent" on one or all of these. "Objective" may also mean "a possession including an activity of an object, or an object itself," as "subjective" may mean "a possession including an activity of a subject, or a subject itself." In value theory, objectivism sometimes is the doctrine that values are objective in the first sense, and that judgments or assertions about values also are. "The proposition that ethical judgments are objective, therefore, besides asserting that they are judgments, asserts of them a certain independence of the feelings or attitudes of the person judging." Also subjectivism in value theory sometimes is the view that values and assertions or judgments about values are dependent on attitudes or feelings, or lack independence of them.[1] In this first sense of "objective" and "objectivism," however, some values that we have already called subjective are objective. Thus, in a certain situation dieting may be

---

[1] A. C. Ewing, *The Definition of Good* (New York: Macmillan Co., 1947), p. 2 and Chap. I.

good for a person's physical appearance or bodily health, and this value of the dieting and the judgment asserting the value may be independent in certain respects of the feelings or attitudes of the person, who may hate dieting, as well as similarly independent of other judging individuals. Hence, the value of the dieting, and the judgment asserting it, would be objective in the first sense, although in the sense we have adopted, the value at least would be subjective, since dieting here is an activity of the subject in the situation, and its value therefore a possession of a subject's activity.

To maintain consistency in our terminology, we shall use the word "objective" primarily in the second sense. The first sense of "objective" will be retained, but as descriptive not of values but of judgments, assertions, analyses, and other forms of cognition that are unbiased or independent of the whims and inclinations and wishes of the individual. Especially will this sense of "objective" be used in the discussion of domains and value sciences later. To parallel the retained second sense of "objective," as descriptive of values, objectivism will mean that in the value situation value is simply an object, or a quality, property, activity, or other possession of objects, and as a complete value theory, objectivism will further mean that value in the situation is independent of the (finite) subject who discovers it by intuition or direct inspection and who acquires his own value from it.

In one form or another, objectivism in this general sense has been advocated throughout the history of Western philosophy. Perhaps, its first major statement was Plato's doctrine of the Idea of the Good, wherein value or good is an independent Form to be apprehended if at all as an object of a supreme intuition. The values of finite things are derived from "participation" in the objective realm of forms. This Platonism was continued in medieval philosophy where the Idea of the Good was replaced by the personal God of Christian theology. It was further extended in modern philosophy by objective idealism from Hegel to Bradley in which the Absolute became the principle of individuality and value.[2]

In more recent philosophy, where the theological and cosmological frameworks of past theories have been dropped, objectivism in value theory is probably most commonly associated with certain British epistemological "realists," notably G. E. Moore and W. D.

---

[2] Cf. Bernard Bosanquet, *The Principle of Individuality and Value* (London: Macmillan Co., 1912).

Ross. G. E. Moore conceives good as "a simple, indefinable, un-analyzable object of thought by reference to which it [the subject-matter of Ethics] must be defined," and also as "that quality which we assert to belong to a thing, when we say that the thing is good." Furthermore, good is a *simple* objective quality like yellow, that must be apprehended directly or intuitively; and the conception of it is incapable of demonstration or explanation to anyone who does not already know it directly. "My point is that 'good' is a simple notion, just as 'yellow' is a simple notion; that, just as you cannot, by any manner of means, explain to any one who does not already know it, what yellow is, so you cannot explain what good is."[3] W. D. Ross supports Moore's general contention that value is a simple quality of objects, and, in the case of "right," a self-evident quality "in the sense that when we have reached sufficient mental maturity and have given sufficient attention to the position [asserting this quality of the object] it is evident without any need of proof, or of evidence beyond itself." But he holds that "good" is a consequential quality, "that it is a quality which anything that has it can have only in virtue of having some other characteristic."[4] However, in both Ross and Moore there is a vein of subjectivism, since the objects that in supreme form have the quality of good in their sense are for Moore "personal affections and aesthetic enjoyments,"[5] and for Ross "states of mind,"[6] both of which usually exist, in the

---

[3] G. E. Moore, *Principia Ethica* (Cambridge: Cambridge University Press, 1903, 1954), pp. 21, 9, 7.

[4] W. D. Ross, *The Right and the Good* (Oxford: Clarendon Press, 1930, 1955), pp. 29, 88; see also pp. 121-122.

[5] G. E. Moore, *Principia Ethica*, p. 189: "personal affections and aesthetic enjoyments include *all* the greatest, and *by far* the greatest, goods we can imagine." Italics in text.

[6] W. D. Ross, *The Right and the Good*, p. 122: "good is a characteristic belonging primarily only to states of mind, and belonging to them in virtue of three characteristics—the moral virtue included in them, the intelligence included in them, and the pleasure included in them." Some recent objectivists would emphatically deny the vein of subjectivism in Ross and in Moore, holding that value is entirely nonprivate and nonpersonal, and certainly never lodged in states of mind. See E. Jordan, *The Aesthetic Object* (Bloomington, Ind.: Principia Press, Inc., 1937), Chap. V and *passim*, and also *The Good Life* (Chicago: University of Chicago Press, 1949). Paul Tillich, writing about N. Hartmann, says "According to Hartmann, values are powers with laws of their own. They have a character of being, standing against the desires and interests of the subject who experiences them as values." *New Knowledge in Human Values*, ed. by A. H. Maslow (New York: Harper & Bros., 1959), p. 192. Cf. E. Vivas, *The Moral Life and the Ethical Life* (Chicago: University of Chicago Press, 1950).

value situation, as possessions of the subject, although, where the objects are human beings, may also exist in objects.

Since our topic is the analysis of human values, the discussion of that type of objectivism which conceives value as residing primarily in some transhuman being, a Platonic Form, God, the Absolute, is outside the main line of our argument. However, some incidental notice of this view will be taken in our discussion of the total human situation later on, particularly the bearing of the transhuman on human value. Meanwhile, perhaps a fair statement of value objectivism that separates it specifically from value subjectivism in the sense discussed in Chapter III, and draws upon Jordan and N. Hartmann and the tradition they continue, and also on Moore and Ross, might be this: in the human situation, value is an object or a property of objects, and discovered there by the subject and not made by him, particularly not by his cognition of it, and, further, all other human values, such as subjective values, are derived from objective value and even reducible to objective value, being obtained by "participation" of human subjects in it. Thus, in eating food or participating in a political or educational institution, value resides primarily in the food or the institution or in various of its qualities, and the values in the eating or participating, these subjective values, are dependent upon the food or institution, and their value quality is determined by the value quality of the food or institution. Not only is eating or participating not even possible without the food or institution, but with a poisonous food or institution, eating or participating is poisoning, or has this negative value, and so on.

This view, reversing subjectivism, which derives the value of objects from the feelings, satisfactions, and attitudes of subjects, is, I think, a very salutary corrective to the exaggerations of its opponent, and very instructive in certain positive ways, as we shall see. But as a complete theory of value it has two rather evident defects.

A great many subjective values, such as health, admittedly are possible only by availing oneself of values in objects—for example, in food. But equally these subjective values are possible only by the actions and resources of subjects. To preserve his health, the ordinary person of course needs good food or to "participate" in the values of appropriate foods. But he must also consume and digest these foods, if not know and select them, and this effort is just as much a causal factor in the subjective value as the qualities of the food. A person with the most wonderful food in the world before him, but too lazy to eat it or too indisposed to digest it, is not going to preserve his health by virtue of the food. The subjective value of health here is possible only by virtue of certain actions of the subject, not merely by the food. Furthermore, this subjective value, a sense of well-being, not only is not caused merely by useful objects such as food, but it is not literally in these objects. Human health or a sense of human well-being is literally in individual sentient human beings only, and not in food at all. In other words, subjective value is *additional* to whatever values may be found in objects, and although it may be related, it is not reducible to these values without remainder, being something more. Indeed, it constitutes a distinct and unique genus of value with characteristics all its own, which were described in the preceding chapter.

Objective value, then, is neither the sole determinant of subjective value, nor does it actually include it, and therefore, value objectivism in its claim that all value not *prima facie* objective is derived from and reducible to objective value is defective in these respects as a complete value theory. Nevertheless, as I have mentioned, the objectivist theory has considerable merit, especially today when the prevailing tendency is, as it has been for many years, to conceive value solely in subjective terms. As we have indicated, and will try to indicate further, objectivism stakes out a unique region of value; and in calling our attention to this region, it makes an important contribution to our understanding of value.

Some general characteristics of this region and of its constituents now require comment.

Some Characteristics

The region of objective values is very large. It includes at least the values of all things and beings in extrahuman nature as objectively related to human beings and human value situations. It also includes the values of all works of the fine and industrial arts, and numerous additional human products such as works of science.

From a certain large cosmological point of view, the things and beings in extra-human nature—trees, sun, earth, animals—might be conceived as subjects, as centers to which other things are value related or to which certain other things have what Laird has called a "natural election."[7] Value might be said to be immanent in these things as subjects, in the manner of Spinoza who defined perfection or value as the amount of reality in anything, its inner strength,[8] or in the manner of Whitehead, who wrote: " 'Value' is the word I use for the intrinsic reality of an event."[9] This larger cosmological view, in which extra-human things are subjects, may ultimately be the only correct view in value theory in full scope. But since our present analysis is concerned with human beings and human subjects, extra-human things in nature or elsewhere will be considered only as objects and not as subjects independent of being human objects. However, what we have said and will say of human subjects, properly modified, may well apply to all these things as subjects, and certainly the possibility of their being subjects is not denied, nor even questioned.

One characteristic of objective values deserves immediate emphasis. The limitation of them to human values does not convert them into dependencies of human subjects. To exist in a human value situation does mean to exist in interdependence. But to exist in interdependence does not mean to exist in one-way dependence. An objective value is the adequacy of the object to meet telic requirements. Except where the human subject manipulates or in other respects does more than evaluate the object, its adequacy depends upon its inherent native strength. It is not imposed but discovered in the evaluative process. Even when this may seem otherwise, for example, when one lowers the telic requirements

---

[7] John Laird, *The Idea of Value* (Cambridge: Cambridge University Press, 1929), pp. 92 ff.

[8] B. Spinoza, *Ethics* (New York: Dover Publications, Inc., 1951), p. 83, Pt. II, Def. VI; *passim*.

[9] Alfred North Whitehead, *Science and the Modern World* (New York: Macmillan Co., 1925), p. 136. R. S. Hartman may have had in mind an analogous view of value in his definition of good: "A thing is good if it fulfils the definition of its concept." "Value Theory as a Formal System," *Kant-Studien*, Band 50, Heft 3 (1958-59), p. 295, see also in Maslow (ed.), *New Knowledge in Human Values*, pp. 13-37. But Hartman's view seems too formal to yield any concept of value at all. Thus, one's definition of a tennis player may be "a person who plays the game of tennis" and of a murderer, "a person who commits the crime of murder." Many human beings "fulfill" these definitions, but this fulfillment does not seem to be what is meant by calling a tennis player good and is more nearly what is meant by calling a murderer evil.

upon failure of the object to meet the initial ones and finds the object satisfying, what has happened is not that the object's adequacy is created but that attention has shifted from certain inadequacies to certain adequacies. The "new" adequacies are immanent properties, as the "old" inadequacies were. Both belong to the independent nature of the object.

Of course, in an interdependent setup this independence is not all. There is also dependence. Things could not explicitly exhibit objective human values unless there were human subjects. There would be no situation or context for exhibiting them. Nor would the great galaxy of objective values that results from the reworking of natural material into human creations exist in independence of human effort. In these respects objective values in the present sense depend on subjects. However, the dependence in these respects is certainly matched by a reverse dependence of subjective values on objects. Indeed, almost all subjectively valuable human acts from breathing fresh air to creating a great artistic or political design, are possible through objects.

Subjectivists who admit this last point sometimes try to minimize it by describing objects here as mere instruments. This characterization may seem just for objects in a certain type of situation. But it fails to cover objects in other instances, and in the end fails to do justice even to objects in the instances apparently covered. The obvious instances not covered are those where the subject, not the object, is a means or instrument. In the great performing artist, in the great teacher or scientist, and in the fields of dedicated human endeavor generally, the overriding consideration usually is to bring out values in the objects. The values in the music or drama, in the object matter being taught or investigated, are the end, and the subject is the means to bringing these values out, and the means-end relationship is the reverse of what it is in the instances commonly cited by the subjectivists. The more complete account, however, is that ideally in *any* value situation the means-end relationship is reversible. Objects may be instruments, a motor car or tree may, as subjectivists claim. But in any such situation, the subject may be an instrument, for example, to show off or develop the values in the tree or motor car. Moreover, this kind of reciprocity seems exactly what we would expect ideally in a relational setup when the full value potential of the situation is adequately developed.

This discussion of the instrumental character of objects leads to the more general question of the exact application of "instrumental values" within the realm of objects and the possible application of "intrinsic values" there. We noted that these types of value exist in the field of subjective values. The question is to determine in what sense if any they may exist, along with other types, in the field of objective values.

Types

"Instrumental" or "extrinsic" contrasts with "terminal" or "intrinsic," but it has two senses as applied to objects and objective values. As just mentioned, ideally all objects and objective values may be subjectively instrumental. They may be instruments of pleasure, power, or other subjective aims. However, as we also noted, objects and objective values may be terminal or ends. Then "instrumental" is applied to them in a second sense to contrast with this sense of terminal. In this context, "instrumental" means the values of any object (or aspect) as means to another object (or aspect), for example, the value of a machine for shaping a tool, or the belt on a machine for turning a wheel on it. Our two senses of "instrumental" correspond roughly to C. I. Lewis' distinction between "inherent" and "instrumental,"[10] or, more precisely, to the distinction between the subjectively instrumental and the objectively instrumental. It is this second sense of "instrumental," of one object being of instrumental value to another, and the corresponding sense of "terminal" that concern us here.

"Terminal" in this sense refers to the values intrinsic to an object (or aspect) taken, not as a means to a subject or another object (or aspect), but as itself an end-point of attention and purpose. Among the more obvious examples of this application of the term are the values of works of art (or of aspects of works of art) in certain contexts. Thus, a work of art (or aspect of one) may be taken as the end-point or focus of an aesthetic experience. In such experience, the aim is simply to perceive the being and values of the work (or aspect) within the outlines of the work itself (or

---

[10] C. I. Lewis, *An Analysis of Knowledge and Valuation* (La Salle, Ill.: Open Court Publishing Co., 1946), p. 391. Except where it is explicitly stated otherwise, Lewis' "inherent values" are included in what we call "instrumental values in the usual subjectivist sense," inherent being the subjectively instrumental.

aspect). The values within the object (or aspect) are preeminently the termini of the act of perception, and nothing beyond the object (aspect), subjective or objective, except as it bears on its internal being, is considered.[11] Or, again, in the creation of a work of art, wherever, or insofar as, the artist aims simply to make the object as resplendent with internal perceptual values as possible, these values are the end-points of the artist's endeavor and purpose, and might therefore be properly called objective terminal values.[12] Other examples are to be found in works of pure mathematics or pure science, indeed in any of the works of man, which are created to possess values in their own right additional to their instrumentality to other things, or which are approached simply to discern the values internal to their independent objective being.

It may be objected that in human activity the goal is never such values, but the consummations (subjective values) gained through them. In aesthetic experiences, for example, the goal is not the values in the object but the having of a certain kind of experience from perceiving these values. The aesthetic object might be called the goal object but it is not the goal, and only the goal or subjective consummation has terminal stature, the goal object functioning primarily as a means or instrument of it.[13]

This objection expresses well the prevailing subjectivist view of objective values. It also describes correctly the primary goal of human activity in innumerable cases. Thus, to use an example of Pepper's when one is hungry and seeking food, the dominant goal ordinarily is not so much food as the appeasement of hunger by the food, and the object is usually sought merely as a means to this end. But even in such cases the values of the object may not be altogether lacking in terminal character. The inference that an apple is edible, or that it has the required instrumental values, may be based on apprehension of certain aesthetic properties, for example, the quality of its color, its size, its texture. Noticing such values may be incidental and on the way to an inference about

---

[11] D. W. Gotshalk, *Art and the Social Order* (Chicago: University of Chicago Press, 1947, 1951; New York: Dover Publications, Inc., 1962), Chap. I.

[12] *Ibid.,* Chap. II.

[13] Stephen C. Pepper, *A Digest of Purposive Values* (Berkeley and Los Angeles: University of California Press, 1947), pp. 24 ff., and *The Sources of Value* (Berkeley and Los Angeles: University of California Press, 1958), Chap. 9.

edibility. But these values *are* intrinsic to that object, elements of its nature, and when one is not too ravenous, they may even be arresting termini, interrupting the flow of activity toward the alleged primary goal.

Besides this remark, and the remarks already made to indicate the independent character of objective values, the above objection requires the following comment to relate it properly to our argument.

While the *main* goal in many cases of human activity, indeed in all instances of so-called "practical" activity, may be a subjective consummation, in many other cases this goal is incidental and the terminal values in the object are central. As I have indicated, I believe this is true in the best examples of aesthetic experience, where the great aim in the experience, as widely recognized, is simply an overwhelming concern for the object—to apprehend what it is intrinsically—and where all thoughts of self are set aside since they would be a disturbance to the experience.[14] Indeed, it is even more the case, I think, in all types of important creative activity, when the artist or creator generally is seeking to build a certain individual whole. While the satisfaction and joy in such work may be very great where the work is successful, these are not usually the crucial concern. Rather it is that the work actually have imbedded in it the value properties that have come to be what the creator wants to see imbedded in it. The object or the resident values of the object are the crucial terminal concern during the activity itself. In any case, such examples make clear I think that objects may be rightly described as having terminal values, even if one also insists upon interpreting as (subjectively) terminal the incidental consummations or satisfactions of the individual subject involved.

Additional to extrinsic or instrumental values for subjects, then, objects have intrinsic values, and these values are intrinsic not as subjective consummations—the only sense of intrinsic that subjectivism allows, but as possessions of objects terminal for the telic pattern or a telic pattern of an activity situation. As to the values of the polar components of human situations in full scope,

---

[14] Compare any "classical" description of this experience, for example, "Psychical Distance," by E. Bullough, in Melvin Rader, *A Modern Book of Esthetics* (New York: Holt, Rinehart and Winston, Inc., 1960), 3rd ed., pp. 394 ff.

they are obviously various, even judging from the few examples already cited. In most cases, I think, they consist of a combination of subjective and objective values, one being instrumental and the other terminal, or both so, depending on the emphasis and complexity of the situation's telic structure.

Of the second sense of instrumental (extrinsic) described at the beginning of this section as corresponding in the object field to the sense of "terminal" or "intrinsic" just considered, perhaps it might be useful to distinguish two different types, in addition to the three C. I. Lewis has already distinguished.[15] First, an object (X) may be said to have instrumental value when it is useful to deal with another object ordinarily existing separate from it (Y), for example, a crowbar being used to pry loose an iron molding, or a bulldozer to cut a road through rough terrain. This is one of the most common meanings of "instrumental" in the object field, I believe, combined with one or more of the three types enumerated by Lewis. Second, an object may be said to have instrumental value in the object field when it is useful to a whole of which it is a part or to other parts of this whole, for example, in an animal a vital organ such as the heart, whose action is useful to lungs and to the entire living being of which it is a part. This second type of "instrumental" is illustrated in other areas besides the organic or life-field, for example, the aesthetic. Thus, the material of a statue (marble, plaster, bronze, wood) with its color, texture, sheen, may subtly affect the aesthetic quality of the form or expression of the statue, and be instrumental—in some cases even more than the form or expression—in determining the aesthetic quality of the whole, so that one may "feel" altogether differently about a statue in marble and an identical figure in pink plaster. The material with its properties, as in the statue, would be an integral part of this whole, not a separate existent, like a crowbar.

---

[15] Lewis, *An Analysis of Knowledge and Valuation*, p. 384, where he writes that predicating instrumental value of object A "may have any one of three meanings: (1) it may be implied that B (or some eventual Z to which B in turn is instrumental) has intrinsic worth; (2) it may be implied that B (or some eventual Z) is sometimes *judged* to have intrinsic value—whether correctly or incorrectly; (3) there may be no implication that B (or any eventual Z) either has or is thought to have intrinsic value." Italics in text. That intrinsic value means subjective value for Lewis and is extended to objects by us, does not affect the possibility nor the validity of distinguishing these three types of "instrumental" values.

But in relation to the whole as well as to the form and expression, from which it is also not separate in existence, it would be a medium or means, that is, an instrument, and have instrumental values. Here again this meaning of instrumental may be combined with any one or more of the three meanings enumerated by Lewis.

Besides terminal (intrinsic) and instrumental (extrinsic), it is important to recognize another division of values in the object field: natural and cultural. Some philosophers have denied this division, claiming that any thing that becomes an object of human attention is *ipso eo* a part of culture, and since all objects of human subjects are of this type, all of them and all objective values are cultural. Of course, if one wishes to use the term "cultural" in this very broad sense, then nature being an object of continuous human attention is by definition part of culture, and natural entities are cultural objects. Still, an important distinction would remain. This is between objects created or appreciably shaped by human art or action, and objects not so created nor shaped. An automobile, a garden, a painting would be a cultural object in this sense, while an unworked iron deposit, a wild forest, or a virginal landscape would be a natural object.

Distinguished in this way, these types of objects are important in several ways for understanding values in the object field.

First, the distinction between natural and cultural objects makes even clearer the limits of subjectivism in value theory. The realm of objective values itself already sets up these limits. But to distinguish within this realm a subregion of objects of value entirely uncreated and unshaped by human action and art, and thus altogether independent of human "practical" will, is by its reference to volitional independence to erect an additional strong barrier against the view that values consist solely of or depend solely upon subjects or subjective factors.

Second, marking off objects with values not in any way predetermined by human will, the distinction also helps to clarify one "popular" meaning of "chance" applied to human life and good. When we go on a Sunday picnic, and the weather is excellent, we sometimes ascribe the good weather to chance, or luck—"having Joe along." In cases where we choose Sunday because we learn from meteorological predictions that the weather will be fine then, we may think we have eliminated chance in the present sense. But even if weather predictions were infallible, and a person based his action on them, the control provided would really be of the time for the action, and not of the prevailing weather. The weather itself would still remain wholly or in large part (barring artificial weather production) at the mercy of nonhuman factors, and, in that sense, a matter of "chance." So much of life involves the mixture of these two types of objective values, values determined by human action (choosing Sunday) and values determined by nonhuman factors (good weather on Sunday), that it is often difficult to untangle the two, like the mixture of inherited and acquired factors in personality. A rule "popular" with some people is to claim all positive values to be the result of human action and all negative values to be the result of chance (nonhuman factors). But, except for a golfer looking for an alibi, this method is not very satisfactory, even subjectively, as a substitute for the more laborious method of studying each instance, and trying to disentangle the part resulting from human causal efficacy, and the part not directly created or shaped by human action.

Finally, an exploration of these two types of objects, the natural and the cultural, might give salutary impetus to a reconception of one of the most central aims or ideals of human striving. This concerns the goal of "culture," specifically our own culture, a very large topic which we can only glance at in passing. Usually, in our society, "culture" is greatly extolled, and many accept already cultured objects as the proper and only concern of human existence. Yet nature is so vast, and its forces even in tiny particles are so powerful, that in comparison culture seems a small and fragile thing. A reconception of the aim of culture that is less self-centered and inbred seems needed if culture is rightly to retain a strong centrality in value thinking.

On such a reconception, the activities of domains constituting a culture (art, industry, science, commerce, family life, and the like) would be described as fundamentally efforts to tame the forces of nature, to develop nature's values into culture-extending values, and to transform natural objects into appropriate cultural objects. According to this view, each domain would have an open door on nature, for example, fine art in the materials it uses, sound, paint, stone, even though some of these materials have been already transformed by pre-artistic treatment. Similarly, with other domains: at least some trace of natural origin would be understood as adhering to its objects. The effort in each such domain would be to renew and extend the transforming of nature already begun, and seek new and ever diverse ways to enlarge the empire of culture *in* nature.

If such a reconception were seriously entertained, one great advantage would be that scientific technology would shed the alarming uniqueness that some people ascribe to it. It would become simply a special case of cultural activity arising out of certain peculiar intellectual and social developments in the West, to be judged by the same kind of intrinsic and extrinsic scrutiny to which other domains are subjected. Scientific technology is commonly regarded as *par excellence* the transformer of nature. But if all domains were similarly conceived, scientific technology would be put in a context where it could be understood not as a disrupting and debilitating anticultural force à la Spengler but as one of many cultural activities in principle alike, and such a perspective might foster a fresh and more balanced appraisal of its status, and of the place of all other types of human activity.

Principle

In this chapter up to this point, we have proceeded as if objects universally had natural or cultural, intrinsic or extrinsic, and, generally, positive objective values. However, this is not precisely the case. In discussing subjective values, we said that subjective activities and states—achievements, satisfactions, even personality—do not as such have value. Only achievements, satisfactions, personalities that meet certain specifications do. This is also true of objects. They have value in fulfilling the requirements of a principle, or in meeting certain specifications, and their value consists of this.

Since the principle of value, according to our account, is relational, this point leads directly to a discussion of the relational component of the value situation. I would like, however, to consider first a paradox connected with this fact and already implicit in the discussion of subjective values. We have classified subjective values as well as objective values as intrinsic (and extrinsic). How can these or any values be intrinsic on a theory that claims the principle of value to be relational? Does not the very notion of relationality mean that no subject or object as a center of value exists in itself. Yet what are intrinsic values if they do not exist in things independent of other things or as things in themselves?

The resolution of this paradox permits us to emphasize an important aspect of the distinction between the subjective and objective and the relational. Our theory is not that relations or the relational constitutes value or is the value of subjects or objects. It is rather that the relational, among other things, is the principle of evaluation. Values are one thing, the principle of evaluation is another, and it is values, or some of them, that are intrinsic, and the principle of evaluation that is relational. Thus, in saying that subjective acts and attitudes or objective events and things have intrinsic value, what is meant is that these items by virtue of their own being in the value situation satisfy certain requirements, and that this satisfying of requirements can be found in the items simply by clear-headedly applying the proper principle to what is in the items without considering them as instruments of other items, subjective or objective. The value, or the being-up-to-the-require-ments, is terminal to the items themselves. However, the principle that tests the value and grades the items is not itself one of the items, a subject or object, but a requirement or demand made upon them. And it is this that is provided by the relational element.

V

RELATION

Relationism

In value theory, relationism has several meanings which are analytically distinct, although they may be combined into one theory. Relationism is the view that values occur only in certain relations,[1] or that values are a result of relations or of a certain relation,[2] or that values are relations.[3] Our own view is not identical with any of these, nor with any combination of them, although it agrees with the first theory in certain respects, as we shall see.

In holding that values occur only in certain relations called transactions, this first theory usually wishes to confine values entirely to the human or animal situation. This procedure is admirable as a methodological rule for focusing discussion on human values, and to this extent we share it. But as an ontological theory it has certain shortcomings. We have already hinted that values may exist entirely outside the human or even animal situation, and although

[1] John Dewey, "The Field of 'Value,'" in *Value: A Cooperative Inquiry*, ed. by Ray Lepley (New York: Columbia University Press, 1949), pp. 64 ff., particularly, p. 69.

[2] Ralph B. Perry, *General Theory of Value* (Cambridge: Harvard University Press, 1926, 1954), pp. 115 ff. See also H. N. Lee, in Lepley, p. 409.

[3] Perry, *General Theory of Value*, pp. 122 ff.; cf. E. T. Mitchell, "Values, Valuing, and Evaluation," in Lepley, *Value: A Cooperative Inquiry*, pp. 190 ff., also, p. 363.

it is not part of our present undertaking to discuss this view in detail, its possibility cannot be lightly set aside.[4] Certainly, if value consists, as we hold, in meeting certain telic requirements, and if telic beings are not limited to human beings nor to higher animals, but in a certain sense include physical and all types of being,[5] value might exist even if no animal or human being existed.

However, the main aim of the first theory on its negative side, I believe, is not so much to limit value to human and higher animals as to protest in the human field against a certain view of objective intrinsic values which conceives these values as absolutes, existing in themselves, isolated from the flux of human existence, transempirical Platonic forms. And on the whole this protest seems justified. At least, our own view is that a human value is the property of meeting certain human telic requirements. Hence, no human value is a thing in itself, or an absolute that can exist out of all telic relations to human beings and the flux of their requirements.

To this remark, however, we should like to add two others. The view of objective intrinsic values protested against by this first version of relationism is not the only one possible. In the discussion of objective values, we described a different version of "intrinsic." According to it, "intrinsic" means not an absolute isolated from human existence but a value found in an object taken as the end-item of a telic pattern. "Intrinsic" means "terminal," as when we look into a work of art and find what is there valuable as a terminus. Here the principle of evaluation is relational, the demands of the *telos*, but the value itself is residential and found in the object taken not as a means to some subject or other object but as an entity good in itself or good in its own right. Such intrinsicality clearly has nothing to do with the value being a transempirical Platonic absolute existing apart from human requirements. Thus, to reject the protested view of intrinsic values, as we do, is not to reject objective intrinsic values, as we do not.

Furthermore, on our theory some human values may exist outside the knowledge of any given human subject or any known

---

[4] Cf. John Laird, *The Idea of Value* (Cambridge: Cambridge University Press, 1929), Chap. III, "The Principle of Natural Election."

[5] D. W. Gotshalk, *Structure and Reality* (New York: Dial Press, Inc., 1937), Chap. VI.

human consciousness. The ability to destroy a human disease germ may exist in a substance long before this substance has been discovered or used by any human being. Could a human value exist forever totally outside the orbit of human consciousness? Certainly, none could be specifically known to do so. But even if a human value could so exist, it would not be totally isolated from human existence. In a relational world, such as we live in, every item has *some* relation to everything else.[6] Hence, a value that never entered into the orbit of human consciousness would still be in some relation to human existence, and might even contribute to its purpose and support. If it seemed helpful to distinguish actual from possible values, one might say that any item capable of meeting the demands of a human *telos* has possible value, and any item meeting these demands has actual value. On this view the crucial point for an item to have value would be its actually meeting or its being capable of meeting the demands of a *telos*. And an item may possess either of these properties, or have value, even if it were not known to do so.

The second version of relationism, that objects are "invested with value"[7] by a relation to human interest, has been discussed in connection with subjectivism, and, in its straightforward meaning, it seems plainly wrong. No matter what we may wish, desire, or hope regarding an object, nor how strongly we may favor it, we cannot invest it with value if it does not have a certain nature. Merely by interest alone we cannot make a silk purse out of a sow's ear, nor confer on a fancy the value of a fact. In the value situation, interest is important, but, generally, it is not itself creative of an object's nature. And unless an object has a certain nature it cannot have certain values, however powerfully it is related to human interest.

Finally, according to our view, values are not relations understood as features in the value situation analytically additional to subjects and objects, as the third version of relationism appears to claim. Such relations have value, or some of them may have. But so do some subjects and objects, and value therefore seems more properly described as a property of all the items in the value situation rather than the relation between some or all of them. Of

---

[6] *Ibid.*, Chap. VII.

[7] Perry, *General Theory of Value*, p. 115.

course, if this third theory means merely that human value is a relational property, or is a property of items as related to certain telic requirements, it is identical with our own view. But if it means something else, and specifically, that value is *the* relation of subject to object in the value situation, this is not our view, and it seems to be untrue, since the relation of subject to object exists in the value situation when the object or the subject has disvalue as well as value, and hence it cannot of itself constitute without supplementation the value of the object or subject there.

From what has just been said and from previous discussions, we may summarize for the first time our own full version of relationism. This view is that a telic principle, and, in most ordinary human situations, the goalward relation of subject to object, is both the principle of human value activity and the principle of evaluation of all that is involved in this activity. Let me amplify this summary in two directions.

We have already drawn attention to the primacy of goalwardness or the telic in human life. The human being is congenitally a seeker of ends. This bent is not merely a characteristic of his animal nature, but of his total nature and of all of his activities, including his art and science and other such phases of human culture, all of which are goal-directed or directed toward ends. Looked at from the outside, as by an imaginary celestial observer, human living may seem like life on an ant hill, a complicated and intricate set of causal processes, very local in range, easily erasable without cosmic consequence. But seen from within as an end-seeking endeavor this cosmic inconsequence ranges from the most jubilant hope to the most devastating heartbreak, and includes all the agony and color and deep satisfactions and frustrations that give substance to human life. Incidentally, when we speak of the primacy of the telic we do not mean merely that it is foundational to practical action which, as Kant held, is primary in human life. The contention is rather that in any region of human existence, in practical action but equally in theoretical contemplation, the telic is the underlying principle of the activity, giving it point and direction and drive.

Even more significant for the argument of this book is the other contention of relationism as above summarized, namely, that the telic is the principle of evaluation, and its requirements the key to understanding the concept of value or "good." We have already noted that this view enables one to explain the ordinary conception of good. When a person says, "X is good," X being a taste or smell, a poem or automobile, a downpour or a watermelon, he means that X meets a certain standard. A set of realizations has been required of the object X, and the object has been judged to have achieved these realizations. Furthermore, we have argued, the telic principle is the clew to the truth of such judgments. Whatever emotive, conative, or other subjective factors are expressed by the statement, "X is good," the statement also has a descriptive content, namely it states that X does meet certain requirements. Accordingly, a person who says "X is good" may be quite mistaken, even admit later he was. He may find that X did not actually meet the requirements, or that these requirements in that situation were inappropriate. The main theme of relationism here, as we shall develop it, is that not only the principle of actual evaluation but the principle of good evaluation or of grading the actual values in a situation, is relational, and that "X is good" but also "X is genuinely or really good" is to be determined on a relational basis.

Since this comprehensive theme will be of capital importance for a great part of the argument of the three subsequent chapters, it calls for extensive illustration from the major areas of value, and to this we now proceed.

Objective Area

In the chapter on the object, we noted that sometimes objects and their values are considered merely as instrumental, and that this is the usual way of judging ordinary objects in common life, where we tend to consider houses, stores, kitchen appliances, automobiles as mere means to our convenience and pleasure. This is also, as we have seen, the typical subjectivist way of interpreting objects and the values of objects, namely, in terms of their utility to subjects. By itself, this view presents no difficulties to a relational theory of evaluation. Indeed, in our first chapter, section 4, we used examples of this sort as our first illustrations of relation as an evaluative principle. In general, the relational theory means in such cases that the value of the object is determined by its relation to the vector of the self-centered aim of the subject, and the object is to be judged valuable or not, entirely on this relational basis.

However, the fundamental principle of value on this view is the good of the subject, and, in the end, the good subject. Hence, while the theory of value of objects it entails is welcome insofar as, and inasmuch as, it places objective values on a relational basis, its procedure of turning the problem of objective values immediately into the problem of subjective values or of the good subject makes shorter work of the problem of objective values than our account of objects warrants. Besides having values as instruments of subjects, objects, we have contended, have intrinsic values as objects, and also instrumental values in a second sense, values to each other. And although these values may have a human reference, they raise questions of principle additional to those raised by the instrumental conception of subjectivists illustrated in common practical experience.

A person may say that a painting, Matisse's "The Dance," for example, is artistically a great painting. He may like it very much or get great pleasure from it. But he may not, and perhaps at the time he may not know anyone who does like it or does get great pleasure from it. That is, he may not know that the painting has or has had instrumental value in the usual subjectivist sense. Yet he may make the above statement, and the statement be meaningful. The statement means that for the person the Matisse painting meets the artistic requirements relevant to a painting with exceptional adequacy. For him the painting conforms in indicated fashion to the demand of the painter's art. Whether the person's conception of these demands is altogether valid or not, is not specifically relevant here for our purposes. The point is that the person is making an evaluation of a painting, and this evaluation consists of an estimate of the conformity of the actualities of the painting to the requirements as he understands them of a domain or subdomain of fine art.

Here we come upon a different type of relationality from that contemplated in the usual subjectivist view. The object is no longer considered an appendage of an individual subject but a member of a domain, and it is judged not by the pleasure or satisfaction given to the individual subject but by its accordance with the purpose structure of the domain. Except where one is concerned, as often happens in common life, with primarily personal or transient ends, this, I believe, is a widely employed way of judging objects. At least, it is one way of judging them, and its scope is very extensive.

Of domains we shall say much more in the next chapter. But a general remark seems pertinent to clarify the nature of the object evaluation under discussion. According to the view we shall develop, each domain—art, science, politics, family life, and so on—has a distinctive purpose structure that places certain requirements on the objects that are its members. These requirements, accurately spelled out, define the maximum value possibilities of objects distinctive of the domain, and thus constitute the total set of distinctive value demands relevant to objects as domain members. They supply, therefore, a principle for judging objects that is competent to measure any object completely, in its unique character as a member of the domain. Since domains constitute the various areas of human life, and objects of nature and culture enter human life as members of a domain or several domains, this relational principle is very comprehensive as well as very fundamental for the judging of the values of objects.

The major difficulties to good evaluation, or evaluation of what is genuinely good, when objects are considered as domain members and not as mere appendages of subjects, lie in detailed empirical knowledge. To continue our example, to judge well a work of fine art, a person must know his object and the maximum value requirements that are relevant to such an object, that is, involved in the purpose structure of the field of fine art. If he knows these, he knows what he is judging and the vector principle most fully competent for judging it as art, and he has only to use his knowledge accurately to make as precise and reliable a judgment as possible. This knowledge of objects and vectors is, as I say, a function of detailed empirical study. To know an object and the maximum value possibilities in a field requires exploring the object and discovering empirically the distinctive purpose structure and scope of the field. That such knowledge is difficult to obtain, that in many cases approximations only are the best that can now be obtained, may be true, as we shall see in later chapters. But if such knowledge is obtained, or, insofar as it is, the problem of good object evaluation here presents no further theoretical difficulty. The object to be judged and the principle for judging it are known. Only accurate application of this knowledge is necessary to judge the object in thoroughly competent fashion.

This relational conception of evaluation obviously applies to judgments of objective intrinsic values, for example, judging the artistic or scientific or ethical or other values in an object when it is taken as a terminus, and not as a means to something else. But no difference in principle is involved, I believe, in judging objective instrumental values—instrumental in our second sense. It is true that "instrumental" here sometimes means merely "effective," so that X, a sharp knife, may be judged to have positive instrumental value if it has any of a variety of objective results, for example, cuts out a tumor or cuts a throat. But even here, the object is judged to have this instrumental value because it is a means to an end, albeit a general end that may be judged differently in different particular circumstances. In other cases, where the object is instrumental to another particular object—a knife for preparing a meal or for laying paint on a canvas—the requirements of the domain of the particular object (cooking, painting) would enter, and the object judged on how its operation fitted into these requirements. In such cases, the method would be the same as described above. That is, knowledge of the object and the requirements of the domain, empirically gained, would be the material for effecting the evaluation on a relational basis.

One other case of objective value calls for brief comment. We often say: "This is a good oak tree" or "This is a good specimen of oil shale," when we may be thinking not of the service of these objects to us but of their distinction among objects of their kind. How does this fit into the relation theory? It is true that "oak tree" and "oil shale" themselves are not domains in our sense, which are areas of human activity. But such areas include scientific and technological investigations, and these investigations establish criteria among objects such as oaks and oil rock. Oak trees that flourish, oil rock that is highly productive, are found among other sorts of oak trees and oil rocks, and the qualities or fulfillments that signalize the flourishing oak and the productive rock are noted and set up as requirements of "good" in these object regions. Thus, the relation principle applies here exactly as it applies in the case of a painting. The object is adjudged good because it meets certain specifications, even though the object, unlike a painting, is not primarily the product of human activity but of extra-human biotic and physical forces, and the specifications demanded of it are not requirements of a humanly mediated fulfillment but of a quality fulfillment by extra-human things and creatures.

Subjective Area

In this area, according to some philosophers, the immediate as such—a pleasure, a satisfaction, a subjective state in its absolute being—is the final good. Indeed, it is *the* final good, to which all other goods in the subjective and objective areas are instrumental. The argument is, self-evidence apart, that in the value field there must be some unquestionable and nonrelativist base on which to build, otherwise, the whole edifice of values is without solid foundation. And just as the immediate in cognition forms a hard core of indubitability in knowledge, so the immediate feelings in subjective experience form such a core in the field of values.

Now, very likely, as these philosophers contend, some solid self-certifying principle is needed to ground the value field, or does ground it. But even so it seems doubtful that the immediate feelings of subjective experience can furnish this. To be sure, many people, and not philosophers conspicuously, believe if they feel fine, if a sense of immediate well-being possesses them, the heights have been attained. And one of the many aims of advertisers and other manipulators of public feeling is to try by all manner of means—by appeals to fear, prestige, sex, nostalgia, and so on—to induce these euphoric states, since people then are usually willing to follow whither the manipulators wish to lead. However, the philosophical flaw in this immediacy theory does not consist of any justification it may give to cynical exploitation. It is in its great abstractness. In any concrete actual situation, the subjectively immediate in experience, the feeling state or whatever, is not final or self-certifying. Of any given pleasure or pain, for example, we may rightly ask: is it good? And if the feeling is the pleasure of a criminal or the pain of a puzzled Socrates, we may decide one way; and, if it is the pleasure of a Socrates and the pain of a criminal, we may come to a different decision. Even with a gratuitous satisfaction, a sweet and pleasing odor coming unasked into our presence, when it obtrudes where we are deeply concerned with other matters, it may be a welcome relief or a nuisance. It all depends. The "context" decides. The ambiguity of value-denoting terms is notorious. In one situation "saving" is "economy" and in another it is "avarice." This is because the values of the acts and states themselves, which the terms try to sum up, shift according to the network of relations in which the given acts or states exist or the network of telic demands within which they have concrete meaning.

One can distinguish, I believe, at least two major contexts or situations in which subjective states and actions are evaluated concretely. In one, a subjective act or state is said to be good or bad "generically" or without reference to some specific individual, and in the other the subjective item is said to be good or bad for a specific individual.

The first type is illustrated by countless examples. People say that to rob a neighbor, to overeat, to start a war, to generalize without facts, are bad, while kindness, physical exercise, aid to underdeveloped countries, the verifying of statements, are good. To sort out the practically countless different examples of this type, and to test each here, would be an impossible undertaking. But I believe all of them belong to a single family. While they do not refer explicitly to an individual subject, they refer to some act or state, character trait or character, of the subject side of a domain or several domains. And the principle determining the value or disvalue asserted is generally the purpose structure of this domain (or several).

Thus, "to rob a neighbor" and "kindness" refer to the moral realm, "to overeat" and "physical exercise" to the domain of health and medicine, "to start a war," and "aid to underdeveloped countries" to the political domain, "to generalize without facts" and "to verify statements" to the domain of knowledge and science. And what the above assertions do or claim to do is to affirm a value or disvalue about the act or state in question on the basis of the value requirements of the purpose structure of the domain. For example, "to rob a neighbor" is to violate a certain demand or requirement of the moral life, and "kindness" is to be in accord with such a demand or requirement; "to overeat" is contrary to certain rules of health and "physical exercise" is in accord with such rules, and similarly, with the others. Whether these claims are true or not, and in what sense, we need not consider now. Indeed, to track down their truth or sharpen up what truth there is in them, is one of the tasks of certain special sciences, moral science, medicine, and so on, which we shall mention later. The point here is that these assertions, seen concretely, concern acts or states of subjects in certain subject-object domains, and they get whatever truth or falsity they have from their accord or lack of accord with the value requirements genuinely governing the pertinent domain (or domains).

Many value assertions about acts and states of subjects, however, are different in form and intent from those just considered. A person may remark: "I don't say X (some act, attitude, state) is good generally, but I think it is good in Y's case," Y being a specified individual. This sort of statement has many diverse illustrations, and involves a certain amount of special analysis that we shall turn to in a moment. But its adequate interpretation along relational lines is, I believe, not difficult to see. What the person who makes the statement means is that X (the act, etc.) may not be suitable for individuals generally, but it fits the needs or requirements or purposes of Y, the specified individual, and so is good not generally but in Y's case.

In particular content, however, this kind of statement still remains ambiguous. Indeed, it may have several different meanings. For example, Y may be a politician, and X may be some act allegedly befitting a politician, for example, denying he said something which he did say but which proved embarrassing when printed in the newspapers. In this case, the value statement under discussion may really be about Y as a politician, and its assertion that X (lying) is good in Y's case may mean that X (lying) is good in the case of a politician. Obviously, this claim may be challenged, but, whether successfully or not, the claim concerns the value requirements of the domain of politics, and the accord of Y's act with these. Thus, the above value statement with *this* particular content becomes indistinguishable from the type of domain value statement just considered in this section.

However, the value statement may refer to Y in some exceptional act, such as taking a drug, and may mean that, while this is not good generally, in Y's case it is. In this form, the statement is still ambiguous. Thus, Y may be a drug addict and the statement may refer to him as that. In this case, its truth may be challenged on grounds of health, or of further damage to the person's professional capacities, and the like, and the statement would again be indistinguishable from the types already considered. But Y may be ill, and his taking a drug may be under medical supervision as an aid to recovery. In these circumstances, the specific evaluation of the act would probably be very different, but the general principle would be the same, namely, the requirements of health. Still, a special observation seems called for in regard to instances involving change, development, and growth.

For example, an aesthetically inexperienced person may enjoy a melodramatic painting that would be found inferior if judged rigorously by the appropriate standards of the painter's domain. While the painting may thus violate certain legitimate requirements of objects in its domain, a person might still argue that the enjoyment of it by Y was good. As a step in Y's growth, as a way of going solidly beyond such things, the enjoyment of a melodramatic type of painting by Y now, when he is very young, is just what should be done. It is evident, however, that the argument has not really transcended the type of case already discussed. The emphasis merely has shifted to what is needed for the growth of a certain type of subject in a domain and away from what is required of mature subjects. Indeed, if the person Y were not young and growing but elderly or grown, the above argument for considering the enjoyment good obviously would not apply. Moreover, even if it were argued that a person's full specific needs should be considered the ultimate measure at least for him, an argument clearly questionable unless the person were so absolutely good that the satisfaction of any of his needs would be indubitably good, the evaluation would proceed along relational if not domain lines, since it would be the requirements of the peculiar telic structure of the person that was the basis of valuation.

In a way less controversial than this last, however, I think, the statement that "X is good not generally but in Y's case" may be given a specific and unique content. For example, X may be an alternate way of doing something (or an alternative attitude) preferred and used by an individual, but, as fully as any other, it may be in accord with the relevant domain requirements. There are several successful ways to skin a cat, and just as one may pay a bill by check or cash, so one may walk or talk or conduct a business in one's own peculiar way, yet be entirely in accord with domain requirements. In such cases, since the general requirements of the domain have been met, the quality of the act or attitude in the specific case must be judged on other grounds. Obviously, the proper grounds are the suitability of the way of activity, or the attitude, to the peculiar telic structure of individual Y. Fitting into this, yet not fitting the peculiar structure of certain other individuals with different inheritance, temperament, and constitution, a way of acting or an attitude clearly may be described as good in Y's case, yet not necessarily good generally.

This point suggests an observation about integrity or what is called "being true to oneself" in the good life. It suggests that individual claims and universal principles, temperament and duty, egoism and altruism, being oneself and being a useful member of a domain or of society, are not necessarily antithetical. The difficulty is to distinguish the proper roles of each and not to confuse them or to set them against each other. What is wanted is a personality with a certain developed inner being in harmony with a widely effective social being. Indeed, the good life for the individual or subject—the life with maximum value—might well rest upon such an inner integrity developed with such a social utility. We shall return to this point later.

Meanwhile, we may note that while our examples in this and the preceding section have dealt with objects and subjects and aspects of these, situations and combinations of situations can be equally used to illustrate our theme. Sometimes we describe a situation which a person is in as a "mess," or a career or a sequence of situations as "a success." Obviously, we are doing here what we have said is done in subject and object evaluations: considering the situation or sequence in relation to some standard, and judging it by its meeting or its failing to meet the demands of this standard.

Ultimate Basis

So far, then, we might say, our general position has been that for judging what is good, genuinely good, in objective entities and events, in subjective acts and attitudes, and in situations, the principle is telic and relational: the purpose structure of a domain, the telic structure of the individual, and so on. Incidental yet not unimportant in our account so far has been the point that the apparent conflict between the two relational bases just mentioned, domain and individual, arises usually from claiming for the individual principle what is really for the decision of a domain principle—for example, to say lying is good in Y's case, although not good generally, then explaining this individual exception by saying Y is a politician. Here really the validity of the judgment "Y's act is good" is not the individual principle (Y's telic structure) at all. It rests with the domain principle, that politics requires lying. Of course, if a person said lying is good in Y's case because Y is Y, his claim would be put on a new footing, the uniqueness of Y, and if intelligible, would have to be judged by the individual principle. But it is difficult to see how this claim could be made intelligible, since lying in the ordinary sense, and telling the truth, are forms of social behavior, and therefore do not seem justifiable by reference to only one individual's nature.

While all this, and particularly the discussion at the end of the preceding section, may suggest in a preliminary way that such forms of the relational principle as domain and individual purpose are not incompatible and may be blended in the concept of a good life, the relational principle itself raises a question of great and even ultimate importance that should be considered at once. The relational principle in some form, we say, grades the subjective and objective areas. But what grades the relational principle? What standard proves the principle of the standard?

It is sometimes said that any alleged instance of good can be questioned, and the answer that is given to explain the allegation of good can itself be questioned, and so on *ad infinitum,* generating an endless regress. A person who says "This taste is good" can be asked: "Why do you say that?" And if he answers "because it is pleasant," he can be asked, "Is pleasure good?" and if he answers "Yes" or "Some pleasures are," he can again be asked "Why?" and so on interminably. This regress has sometimes been called the Mountain Range Effect.[8] The only way to eliminate it, some hold, is to give up the attempt at normative justification and accept some other type, such as pragmatic justification,[9] or make the final principle of justification a pure postulate.[10]

In the case of our relational theory, however, wherein we do not put forth some special concept of the good such as pleasure, I believe the difficulty of a regress does not arise, and such desperate remedies as just mentioned, which are said to be needed to avoid it, are not required. To discover a principle for grading our principle of grading we do not have to go outside the principle, and to the question, what principle proves our principle of the standard?, the reply is the relational principle itself. Indeed, any telic principle as a standard has a certain specific purpose or a certain job to do. And it is a good standard, just as anything else

[8] Philip B. Rice, *On the Knowledge of Good and Evil* (New York: Random House, Inc., 1955), pp. 46-47.

[9] *Ibid.,* pp. 153 ff.

[10] Donald C. Williams, "Ethics as Pure Postulate," *Phil. Rev.,* Vol. 42 (1933), pp. 399-411.

is good on our theory, if it satisfies the requirements of this purpose or the demands of the job; in other words, if it lives up to the claims embedded in it. Thus, any relational principle as a standard carries within it its own principle of criticism, and can be graded simply by its success in satisfying demands implicit within the principle itself.

We might state all this less summarily by saying that a telic principle as a standard for judging the value of anything has two functions. The first is to enclose the distinctive value possibilities of what is being judged, an individual as individual, a situation, a domain, and so on. For example, regarding domains, the purpose structure attributed to science or art or politics should plainly have room for the distinctive range of value realizations genuinely possible in science or art or politics. The second function of a telic principle as a standard is to grade the value actualities of the individual, situation, domain, or whatever, in the light of the realization possibilities. Now, a telic principle that is a good standard is simply one that does this twofold job. It marks out the genuine and distinctive value possibilities of the individual, situation, domain, and it shows us on this basis what the values of the actualities in the item are. In doing this, or insofar as it does it, a telic principle as a standard fulfills the purpose of a standard, and thereby justifies itself. It realizes the value possibilities of a standard, or achieves all that a standard by its nature can be asked to do.

On this view, according to which a standard contains its own principle of criticism, we can always ask of any proposed or employed standard: does it do the particular job required of a standard? Does it meet the requirements of *that* purpose? Thus, our relational theory implies that standards are developed and tested by a process of immanent criticism, or, at least, by an immanent principle. Accordingly, no outside or extrarelational principle is needed, and the so-called Mountain Range Effect simply does not arise.

Particularly important to note in this connection is that our telic or relational theory does not require us to retreat to some extra-human territory, and to assume, in the manner of Descartes, that human evaluation requires an imposed idea of Perfection, or an idea of God causally derived from without. The only assumption necessary is what seems to be a fact rather than an assumption, that the human being is a telic being, that he is a fountain of standards.

On such an assumption, all that is needed cosmologically is supplied. In saying this, I do not mean that larger cosmic considerations may not be of greatest importance in further clarifying human standards. On the contrary, such considerations may be of considerable importance, as we shall see. The point here merely is that a firm and bedrock underpinning for human evaluation does not require a special injection from an extra-human being. Human nature suffices. However, our theory is not to be confused with numerous other theories: for example, the view that certain primary aims or drives are imbedded in human nature and all other types of human effort are to be understood as learned responses developed in satisfying these aims or reducing these drives. This is a highly complicated psychological theory of motivation that can be assessed only in terms of detailed psychological evidence that would affect our theory neither one way nor another.[11] Our point is much more general and simple, and briefly it is this. As a telic creature, the human being is a standard-producing agent, and his standards can prove themselves. A good standard is merely one that actually does the job of a standard, and a specific standard is good, not because it has a high cosmic origin, but because it realizes in evaluation the requirements of the principle of a standard—the purpose—inherent in itself.

---

[11] Cf. B. J. Diggs, "Ethics and Experimental Theories of Motivation and Learning," *Ethics,* Vol. LXVII, No. 2 (Jan., 1957), pp. 100-118, for a discussion and evaluation of this theory in light of recent findings in experimental psychology.

VI

DOMAINS

Varieties

A domain is any well-established area of human value activity, or, more specifically, any area of human value activity that has an established and distinctive telic pattern. Such areas are illustrated by art, science, politics, religion, sport, law, education, war, and countless others. Just as purposes in human individuals are so organized that a major purpose often includes a multitude of subordinate purposes, so domains often include subdomains, for example, science includes physics and chemistry, art includes music and poetry. These subdomains are themselves domains, as purposes included under a major aim are themselves purposes, and what we shall say about domains will generally apply also to all of the varieties of subdomains.

Obviously, as we are using the term, a "domain" is not intended to indicate a fixed "metaphysical" division of the universe. Rather it denotes a family of diverse value situations whose members have certain distinctive and settled resemblances. Domains arise as purposes stabilize, and vanish as purposes wither or disappear. They can expand, overlap, and change character. However, insofar as they constitute a domain, each family of activities has its own distinctive purpose pattern. Poetry *is* poetry and not politics, even if it may be very difficult to say what poetry is. Furthermore, like families and their activities, domains themselves have similarities, and settle down into types. To begin a delineation of the varieties of domains, it might be useful therefore to describe some of these types. Also, inasmuch as domains are families of value situations which consist of subject and object components in a purpose structure, it is perhaps easiest to classify the varieties of domains by the nature of their subjects, objects, and purpose structures.

Beginning with subjects, it is sometimes said certain activities belong to the women's sphere, others to the men's, and still others to both. In certain societies, these divisions are very rigid, but in modern Western society, they are rather fluid, and an increasingly large number of domains, once exclusively spheres for men, have become open to women, and vice versa. Again, one might distinguish certain activities as adult, others as children's, and others still as equally both: marriage is for grownups, the nursery for tiny tots, and family life for both.

Of the various divisions of domains made on the basis of the subject component, one becoming increasingly important is based on the type of training of personnel. Some domains require highly specialized training, others not. With the growth of a technological civilization based on natural science, the number of domains of the first type has increased enormously. This has been a great gain in certain ways, particularly in efficiency and technical progress, but it has evident perils. Already it has encouraged a tendency to put important and even life-and-death decisions in the hands of people lacking the broad background and perspective necessary to make them properly. The accelerated channeling of highly talented personnel into narrowly specialized training may develop a race of expert technicians, but obviously it may also develop a race of cultural morons. Particularly is this possibility very real, I think, where the specialized training lacks a context of education and liberal experience in the general scope and variety of value.

Using objects as a basis, domains may also be classified in various ways. Thus, some domains such as ethical activity have human beings for objects. Some do not: electronic engineering, mathematics, and the physical sciences. There are no exact descriptive terms for this division: "human" and "nonhuman" are possibly the best. Yet the difference is real and important.

Objects also differ in tractability, and domains derive generic differences from this. In some domains, subjects can exert considerable control over objects, shaping them according to their wishes. In others, the object is no more controllable than the weather. This difference indeed can be illustrated by that between manufacturing and meteorology: in the one case human planning and action usually shape the object decisively, while in the other case the object (weather) is merely chartered but is as yet amenable to only slight physical or practical control by human beings.

Closely connected with the two object distinctions just made is another that supplies a particularly instructive differentiation of domains. We have already noted that one of the great activities of human beings is the transforming of natural objects into cultural objects, so that a tree, a mineral, and the like are not merely items in nature but can be connected with aesthetic, practical, and other concerns of human culture. Of cultural objects, however, one can distinguish two sorts, roughly but only very roughly described as "real" and artificial, namely, objects found in nature and objects invented or developed by man. If for the sake of illustration we assume that the objects in mathematics are mathematical symbols, and that mathematics is the manipulation of these symbols according to stipulated rules, mathematics would be a domain of the artificial type; while if we assume that the objects of geology are the earth and its component strata and so on, geology would be a domain of the "real" type. In this sense, music, games, town planning, finance, jurisprudence, and all domains in which objects are manipulated after being prepared to be what they are by human beings, would constitute artificial domains. On the other hand, mining, hunting, fishing, many natural sciences, and all domains whose objects are found in nature, although the tools for handling these objects may be human inventions, would constitute "real" domains.

Of course, when such an activity as hunting becomes a "sport," and birds and beasts are bred and released at fixed times and places to serve as objects of the sport, hunting ceases to be a "real" domain. Many domains such as manufacturing and education at lowest level begin, roughly speaking, with natural objects, but for the most part they work with humanly prepared objects, while the objects in no domain, even the most artificial, are altogether lacking in natural properties. The great dividing principle is whether the object in a domain has been prepared to serve as such before it is an object in the domain. Where the object itself has not been so pretreated, as in innumerable activities from primitive fishing to astronomy, the domain or subdomain is of one type, and where it has, the domain belongs to the other.

This division of domains we have described as particularly instructive. For one thing, it suggests the limits of human control over nature and the tremendous distances remaining before the modern "ideal" of domesticating or conquering nature is actualized even in the tenuous sense of putting some stamp of human ingeniousness and invention upon natural entities. The number and extent of objects in the "real" domains is exceedingly large, as we see for example when we gaze for a moment beyond our planet. And many of these objects, not to mention multitudes of them on earth, even when they are imprinted with human art—the moon decorated with an American flag!—are still almost totally beyond human shaping at this time. To be sure, entities so imprinted illustrate the possibility of being so shaped, but even more they illustrate at present the vast problems that any serious concern for the modern ideal of "conquering nature" involves.

Again, objects in the artificial domains show that contrary to unreflective belief objects as such are not foreign bodies, and indeed that some sizable areas of objects are almost wholly products of human contrivance. Finally, the division of domains into "real" and artificial reminds us of the extremes of our culture, which on the "real" side has frontiers where all the spirit of adventure and the hardiness of the pioneer are still needed, and on the artificial side has areas of radical refinement—music, mathematics, even chess!—where human invention has so completely taken over that hardly more than inborn gift is needed, as in the prodigy, to attain extraordinary excellence. It might seem here that Walter Pater's dictum that all arts should approach the condition of music should be extended to the domains of culture, and the growth of culture be conceived as the conversion of "real" domains into such purely contrived ones as are illustrated by music. But, even if desirable, accomplishing such an aim seems very remote, for the activities now devoted to pre-eminently artificial regions are only one small and rarefied segment of human culture.

When we turn to the purpose structure or telic component of domains, we have of course more than another principle of types. We have the principle of domain evaluation, but, more primitively, as we shall see, we have the chief principle of domain differentiation.

However, this component also provides a principle of type division. Of various illustrations, we shall limit ourselves to one of special importance for our analysis, the division into pragmatic and reflective types.

By a pragmatic domain we shall mean one where the subject-object transaction aims primarily at securing or strengthening the individual or group as an effective mechanical agent or causal unit; for example, farming undertaken to gain a livelihood, to grow food and earn money and obtain the wherewithal to live. By a reflective domain we shall mean one where the subject-object transaction aims primarily at strengthening or developing the individual or group in its intrinsic purposive being or as a telic unit; for example, a fine art undertaken primarily for the good intrinsic in the activity or the object.

We should note at once that any pragmatic activity may have reflective good, and any reflective activity may be a means to a livelihood. The difference is merely in the relative weights of these ends, and activity in a domain of one type may shift to the other type by altering these relative weights. Thus, farming might be undertaken primarily out of the love of growing things and for the great interest in watching and tending and developing unusual or rare types of living things, as in "gentleman farming." The gaining of a livelihood would not be the chief aim. When this is so, farming would illustrate exactly what we mean by a reflective domain. Obviously, in its usual form agriculture is not this type of activity, the great aim being to grow and cultivate edible and other causally useful products that yield a livelihood to the farmer and distributor, and give bodily sustenance or useful raw materials to the purchaser. Were agriculture merely a "grow-for-fun" activity and its products of minor use for bodily nourishment and other causal processes, it might exist to some extent, as gentleman farming exists. But it would not be what it is now, nor occupy the kind of place it does in the human economy.

Conversely, painting as a fine art and illustrative of a reflective domain may gain the artist a livelihood. Indeed, painting may exist, as in commercial art, pre-eminently for this purpose. But were painting on the whole primarily this, it would be one more practical art, as some of it is. Painting is considered a fine art because its distinctive purpose and achievement are different. Indeed, painting may be great as fine art, as so much of past painting has

been, yet bring little or no financial return or other causal sustenance to the painter. The measure of the painter's greatness and
of the greatness of a painting as fine art lies elsewhere, specifically
in its intrinsic aesthetic values. These values—in the activity for
the painter, in the object or product for people generally—are the
measure of the stature of the fine art of the painter and the painting,
not the money or the luxuriousness of the livelihood the activity
affords.[1]

To these qualifications, we should add that ideally the aim
in all domains should be both pragmatic and reflective in compatible
amounts. Just as agriculture can have reflective values that become central in gentleman farming, so painting can have pragmatic
values that become central in commercial art. The important requi-
site for maintaining the integrity of a domain as reflective or
pragmatic is that the additional aim be a minor and not the central
determinant in crucial decisions. It should be retained so long as
consistency with the distinctive domain purpose can be maintained,
and excluded only where it interferes with this purpose. Besides
this, two other remarks seem appropriate here about this important
division of domains.

First, in their basic character some domains clearly belong to
the pragmatic or the reflective sphere. Not only agriculture, but
industry, the practical arts, business activity generally, engineering and medicine, are principally pragmatic domains. Despite
the many opportunities for reflective values in all of them, their
primary aim is to sustain and increase the physical strength,
health, and other causal resources of the individual or group. On
the other hand, not only the fine arts but the pure sciences, philosophy in the traditional sense of an activity aiming at wisdom,
religion, and ethical activity in the sense of treating oneself and
others, in Kant's phrase, as ends in themselves, belong primarily to
the reflective sphere. Despite the many pragmatic consequences
that often flow from these pursuits, they are principally efforts
to develop and strengthen man as an inherently purposive being

---

[1] D. W. Gotshalk, *Art and the Social Order* (Chicago: University of Chicago
Press, 1947, 1951), Chap. II, pp. 37-38. In considering an activity or object
as terminal or as the end-item of a telic pattern, our consciousness primarily
turns back upon the activity or object instead of looking beyond it to something else. Also, the values in the activity or object as end are uppermost, and
not those in it as means. Hence the term "reflective."

and activities and objects for their own intrinsic worth. However, there do seem to be domains in which both pragmatic and reflective aims are equally fundamental, notably the school and family life. Both of these have very genuine pragmatic aims, particularly to grow and mature talent able to meet better the causal challenges in individual and group existence. But at their best the family and school can have equally eminent reflective virtues, as major segments in a way of life, delightful in their own right, and among the more memorable areas of human experience.

Second, the division of domains into reflective and pragmatic brings all of the general goals of human activity under two great headings. This result has one very important consequence for clarification of the concept of the good life. It suggests that a comprehensive way of stating the concept of the good life for human beings generally might be as the achievement of an inwardly well-developed people in a mechanically or causally secure world. Such a concept combines into one idea the reflective and pragmatic aims that we have used to classify domains, and gives a single complex meaning to what might otherwise seem to be separate and antithetical purposes. Certain aspects of this concept will come up for discussion later when we actually consider the topic of the good life. Meanwhile, much remains to be said about domains themselves, particularly about their structure and their role in culture. Also, a general observation on an emphasis in our discussion of domains should be made at this point.

In illustrating domains, we have usually mentioned and will continue to mention those rich in positive value possibilities: art, science, agriculture, education, and the like. But it should be understood that, as well-established areas of human activity, domains and subdomains include war, murder, crime generally, and not merely areas rich in positive value possibilities. These areas may properly be called domains both because they are well established and because their activities are goalward or undertaken to gain certain ends, for example, increase in territory, purely bestial satisfaction. That such ends are deficient in value achievement, that they usually entail value destruction far more than value attainment, that they are patterns of evil much more than patterns of good, seems fairly evident. We shall return to this topic in the next to last section below. In any case, to illustrate sufficiently the positive and substantial meaning of domains, repeated citation of these areas hardly seems necessary, although it should be remembered that these areas *are* domains, since they are families of well-established goalward acts, although burdened with vast arrays of disvalue.

Structure

A domain, then, is any area of human value activity that has an established and distinctive telic pattern or structure. I would like now to shift the emphasis in this statement more explicitly to its last term. Better than the other components of value situations, this differentiates one domain from another, or individuates it. Subjects and objects are not in themselves particularly differentiating, passing in and out of domains, usually members equally of several or many. What sets them off as differentiated subjects and objects and as differentiated subject-object wholes is the business that brings them together or the purpose they have with each other. This differentiating purpose structure is often inadequately indicated by a label, which sometimes fits a domain but sometimes does not. For example, politics is a domain, but the term "politics" is often used to mean "partisan intrigue," and in this sense we speak of "politics" in business, education, or family life. In such usage, the term does not denote a domain but a purpose of much wider extent. What differentiates a domain is not a label (usually, however, a domain has a label) but its form, its distinctive telic form.

In some respects, the structure of a domain is like that of any value situation. In both there is an end or telic factor governing the subject and making demands on the object and combining the two into a single unit. What is peculiar to a domain is that its telic pattern is generic or has certain distinctive generic traits. Fine art is not limited to an instance of fine art. Its purpose governs a plurality of instances. At the same time, fine art is not practical politics, no more than painting is negotiating a treaty. The general aim is different, as are the general requirements that the aim places on subject and object. Indeed, if any given domain such as painting did not have a distinctive telic form, it would have no excuse for being as a domain. All of value in it would be included in what some other domain already had in it, and it would therefore be nonexistent as a marked off area of human activity.

In a respect additional to those just mentioned, the structure of a domain is like the structure of a particular value situation. It is the principle of value of the region. Its purpose structure properly delineated encloses the distinctive goal possibilities that can be realized in the domain, what characteristic values can be expected and obtained by success within the area it governs. In doing this, it imposes by implication certain requirements on subjects and objects that must be met if they are to gain or have the good in the region. However, these requirements are not only directions for success. They are also bases for grading the actualities, subjective and objective, in the area. By indicating what values can be the case, the requirements give a basis for determining the stature of the values that are the case. Finally, as with the purpose structure of any particular value situation, that attributed to a domain must meet the requirements of a principle of value itself. It must be a purpose of such scope as to have room for all genuine and distinctive value possibilities or realizations there, thus becoming competent to measure all the genuine and distinctive values that may be attained in the domain.

The delineation in detail of the diverse telic patterns of domains, patterns of good and evil, is a major task of a set of special sciences to be described in the next chapter. But certain general points may be noted here.

First, the requirements of a domain purpose may be realized in many ways. There can be good government in Greece with one set of institutions and in England with a different set of institutions, just as there can be good art in ancient China or in modern France. Hence, in envisaging the structure of a domain, what is needed is a power of abstraction capable of seeing this structure in its full generality. Since the "same" purpose is realizable in many different environments and in many different ways, the relativity, diversity, and plurality implied by "many different" must be allowed in the conception of the "same." Ineffectuality here consists of pitching the concept of domain structure at too low a level. So many English philosophers of great common sense but deficient in philosophic imagination are especially prone to this, being greater friends of the individual and particular, than of the abstract and universal. One might conceive beauty—the general aesthetic value—as a certain proportion, for example, the golden section of Hogarth. The difficulty is that so many things obviously beautiful do not exhibit this proportion or are accounted beautiful for another reason. Like so many other value terms beauty is a summarizing word. What it stands for is an X or set of Xs, for example, qualities possessing for a percipient a high concentration of aesthetic values. Such an X or set is all that is required, not one particular X, such as the golden section. Similarly, the differentiating structure of a domain must be conceived in a generality sufficient for its purpose. Since domains usually cut across historical epochs and national boundaries, their structures must also be conceived so as to possess considerable flexibility as well as generality.

Second, although the principle of a domain is a differentiating structure and its full realization in any instance involves all of the domain's differential value possibilities in a certain particular pattern, this does not imply that these realizations are the only values open to members in the domain in question. It has sometimes been believed that to be different A must be utterly different or have no elements in common with non-A. In the case of domains at least, this is not so. To be different and distinctive, all that is needed is that a domain have *some* uniqueness, not that it be all uniqueness. An excellent work in pure mathematics should have the unique properties of excellence in pure mathematics, but it may (or may not) have values also in physics and other natural sciences. Good government should have the excellences of government, but for that very reason perhaps it may have economic, moral, and other virtues, and even be instructive to science and philosophy. No domain is necessarily (or, it would seem, actually) sealed off from all others. Its only requirement as a distinctive entity is that it not blend entirely into the others or lose all individuality. But in addition to its individuality, it clearly may have many other properties including connections with other domains. It is important, of course, not to confuse these other properties with its distinctive ones. Fine art is often defined as play, wish fulfillment, and the like, and all of these ends may be served by the activities of artists and/or by works of art. But they are not distinctive of these activities or works. In conceiving the structure of a domain, the important step is to place the differentiating purpose first, then to add other value possibilities as, or insofar as, they are compatible with this crucial purpose, and, particularly, interfertilize it.

Third, a few words probably should be said here about a domain and an institution. In a certain general sense, there is no difference between them since an institution might be described as we have described a domain, as an established subject-object area governed by a distinctive general purpose. However, we shall make a distinction, and interpret an institution as an apparatus or agency of a domain, rather than as a domain itself. Thus, natural science is a domain. A research institute devoted to natural science is an institution. Government is a domain. The United States government is an institution. In other words, an institution is a particular agency set up to realize a domain purpose. Also, it is a group agency, or an agency in which a group of individuals operates. Individuals unattached may, however, execute a domain purpose—for example, a scientist. Indeed, early modern scientists often did their work on their own, unattached to any scientific institution.

A domain, then, has a differentiating structure that places requirements upon subjects and objects for attainment of the distinctive value possibilities of its area of activity. This structure makes demands and imposes obligations. It determines what ought to be the case, what is right and wrong. Such concepts as obligation and "ought" are common topics in value theory, and particularly the concepts of right and wrong, and right and good.

Right and Good

"Right" as well as "good" is often given a central position in value theory. It is also regarded sometimes as ultimate and autonomous, not deriving its value-meaning from any other source. An action is held to be right not because it produces good results but on account of its intrinsic character or rightness. This is the view of W. D. Ross regarding moral rightness.[2] On its negative, or anti-utilitarian side at least, this view coincides with our own, which also agrees with deontology generally that the morally right is independent of and incommensurate with "happiness." To say that keeping promises is morally right, *prima facie* right and actually right morally if no stronger right supersedes it, does not mean that keeping promises produces pleasant consequences, although it may produce these. According to our account, it means, if true, that keeping promises fits a requirement in the relations of moral

[2] W. D. Ross, *The Right and the Good* (Oxford: Clarendon Press, 1930, 1955), Chap. II particularly. For a criticism of Ross, and an excellent discussion of deontology with which I believe the main contentions of this section agree, see Oliver A. Johnson, *Rightness and Goodness* (The Hague: Martinus Nijhoff, 1959).

beings. Moral purpose makes this demand, and the rightness of the action is not in its hedonic aftereffects but in its fitting this demand of the purpose structure of the moral situation or domain.

This conception of moral "right" as fitting a demand of moral purpose can obviously be generalized by dropping the adjective "moral." In this form it explains a great variety of uses of "right" as a value term, distinct from right in other senses, as for example, a physical direction (left, right). Of a scientist who has made a certain statement, we sometimes say that he is right, when we mean that his statement is true or coincides with the requirements of knowledge or truth. Or, we say that a scientist did just the right thing in conducting a certain set of experiments, meaning that he did exactly what was fitting to achieve a valued discovery. In fine art, we say that a certain color or shape or line is just right, meaning that it coincides perfectly with the aesthetic requirements of the painting. "Right" is applied not only to acts and attitudes in domains but also to acts and attitudes in their unique bearing on individuals. We say that Jones chose exactly the right wife or job or sport for him. Here what is meant is not so much that Jones's act coincided with the requirements of some domain, which of course it might, but rather that it fitted the peculiar purposive structure of Jones, or all his own peculiar needs and requirements in a certain direction.

"Right" then might be described as a general value term as well as a basic one. Used as an adjective rather than a noun, it can be distinguished from "ought" and also from "obligation" or "duty," if this is desired, by the aspect of the value situation it emphasizes. An "ought" might be described as a requirement itself, an imperative or demand. "Right" as an adjective would then mean "fitting an ought or demand." "To tell the truth," let us say, is a *prima facie* requirement or "ought" of morality. Then, actually telling the truth, this act, is right, *prima facie*, in the moral sense. To go a step further, an obligation or duty might be distinguished as an "active" ought. If in general you ought to tell the truth, then, in a specific situation where you ought, you have an obligation or duty to do so. The obligations or duties of citizenship, art, or science are the requirements or oughts of these value domains in most active, urgent, compelling form. When the scientist (artist, citizen) says his duty is to his science (art, state), he usually means not only that he ought to meet the demands or requirements of this domain, but that this action has a certain precedence and urgency.

"Good" and "right" as adjectives also emphasize different aspects of the value situation. "Right" means "fitting a requirement of the purpose principle of a domain." It refers to what is needed in the value situation if the purpose structure is to be realized. "Good" refers to the realization side of the situation. In subject or object, where telic fulfillment occurs, instrumental or terminal, there *prima facie* is good. Thus, "right" and "good" denote different focuses of the value situation. "Right" refers to its demands; "good" to its fruits. "Right" means fitting these demands: what fits is right. "Good" refers to the realization in subject or object of the purpose itself. Of course, this purpose must itself fit the requirements of a principle of value and satisfy the purpose of this principle, that is, be "right" and "good." But this should be understood here, as I trust it is everywhere, throughout our discussion. Our use of Ross's term *"prima facie"* is intended to emphasize this point.

Perhaps, more than "good," "right" becomes a prominent and more problematic element in the value situation where failure or conflict is actual or possible. Did human life consist of passing easily and peacefully from satisfaction to satisfaction, like a bee gathering honey from an endless series of flowers, everything would be "good," and the concept of right probably would remain submerged. It is only because subjects and/or objects fall below requirements, or tend or threaten to do so, or because situations have conflicting requirements, that the sense of right becomes prominent.

In the individual, the sense of right is called conscience, and conscience certainly seems to become most active where a requirement is or has been violated or threatened with violation, or where the individual is confronted with conflicting claims. The violation or conflict may concern a requirement of the individual purely as individual without consideration of a domain principle, as when a particular person feels that for him with his temperament and talent and training a certain act or choice was or is or would be wrong, however it may be or seem to be for others. Apart from this, I believe, conscience is really concerned with the requirements or alleged requirements of a domain or several domains.

Moral conscience is clearly that. In the individual, moral conscience becomes active when he believes that an attitude or act menaces or disturbs the requirements of morality in the case, or the moral well-being.[3] A writer or painter is said to have an artistic conscience when he inserts into or eliminates from his work certain items that may appear to be optional or inadvisable, but whose omission or presence seems in his eyes to violate what is demanded to do the artistic job honestly. A physicist who scrupulously publishes his experimental findings, although they contradict his previously held theories, is said to show a scientific conscience. Conscience, particularly moral conscience, is sometimes described as the irrational prohibitions and compulsions drilled into one in childhood, reflecting the imperatives of parents and the conventions of society, a kind of "group-think." And in some people conscience is little more than that. But in general it is the sense of right, of what is forbidden and what is required, and obviously this may be based on a rational grasp of the purpose structure of a domain and its demands, as well as on irrational fears and anxieties induced by some dictated or stereotyped version of this structure.

The well-known diversity of opinion as to what is right, as much as the diversity of conscience, also illustrates the general point we are making about "right" and "wrong." A person X may describe the actions of A, the head of a United States Senate investigating committee, as right and characterize A as a "sharp fighter," while another person Y may describe these actions as wrong and characterize A as an "unscrupulous trickster." The difference here may be that X accepts A's purposes and believes his actions fit into what these purposes require, while Y rejects these purposes as, for example, contrary to the purposes of a Senate committee and what these last require. Or, Y may accept A's purposes and believe A's actions violate what they require of him as a senate inquirer. In any case, it is the telic perspective of X and Y and what is required by it that determines their opinion of what is right and wrong here. A similar diversity in this perspective in any field, literary criticism, business, education, religion, can generate a similar diversity of opinion on the rights and wrongs there. Where such a perspective is widely accepted, rules can be set up as conditions of practical activity or induced from instances of practice,[4]

---

[3] Cf. Iredell Jenkins, "The Significance of Conscience," *Ethics*, Vol. LXV, No. 4 (July, 1955), pp. 269-270, *et ante.*
[4] John Rawls, "Two Concepts of Rules," *Phil. Rev.*, Vol. LXIV, No. 1 (Jan., 1955), pp. 3-33.

and a kind of rule morality established. Utilitarianism or the greatest happiness principle has sometimes been thought to provide a broadly acceptable perspective, and rule utilitarianism a suitable *modus vivendi*. Also, wherever these rules are codified as laws, legal positivism has its most convincing exemplification, although the fallibility of the courts, and other internal reasons, such as contradictions between enacted and constitutional law, diminish the strength of such instances.

When courts fail, the problem of right and wrong is not necessarily settled by conscience. It is merely handled in this way customarily, by the group or the individual. What determines right is not necessarily what in all conscience any individual or group believes, but what investigation proves the telic structure of a situation, domain, or individual actually requires. That in our present state of knowledge this telic structure and its requirements are often incompletely known, must certainly be granted. Indeed, what is needed at present is a whole set of new sciences to develop this knowledge, a point which will be a major theme of the next chapter.

"Right," then, is a major property in value situations, while domains themselves, consisting of families of value situations, may be described as constituting what is commonly called the culture of a society. More commonly than "right," however, "evil" is contrasted with "good." Since this contrast has some importance for a theory of domains, and also for a theory of culture, we shall add a few words here to what has already been said about it.

Good and Evil

If good is value realization, evil is value destruction, and patterns such as murder wherein activity is value destructive are prime illustrations of evil. Yet, it seems, no human act is pure evil. Ordinarily, the murderer for example aims at what he thinks is some good, such as revenge, wanton blood-letting, a "thrill." Moreover, what he does, indeed any evil, can be instructive of what evil is. And often the good involved with evil may be very great, as when a war not only successfully defends the freedom of the people of a country but has numerous other fruitful consequences from stimulating farm and factory production to intensifying scientific research.

Frequently acts that are value-destructive are also self-destruc-
tive. Not all of them are. But many acts, for example, those arising
from the overvaulting ambition of Macbeth or the habit of a hopeless
alcoholic, being persistent and sustained, destroy the agent and
bring all his actions and being into ruin. Yet even in such instances,
it might be said, certain tiny value realizations occur, certain purposes are fulfilled, that give a minor tinge of good to what is done.
The self-contradiction of evil is not a pure logical movement, clean
and clear like a mathematical demonstration. It is mixed with impulses complicating the act structure both by their presence and
the minor realizations they add to the experience.

If no act is purely evil, is any act purely good? Are not all acts
a mixture of good and evil? This is not exactly an easy question, but
the answer depends partly on how one takes "an act."

An act considered abstractly and out of context may be good or
evil. In a certain context, a cutting remark may be sheer evil. But
in another situation it may be just what the other person needed to
arouse him to do the right thing. It should be noted, and even
emphasized, that this relativity to context, really to its purpose
structure, does not mean that the meaning of evil varies with the
context. Everywhere and always evil means value destruction. The
relativity refers to the acts, or more accurately, to what purpose
structure they are related to. As related to A, an act may be good,
and to B, evil, for in relation to A the act is a value realization, and
in relation to B, it is a value destruction.

Concretely, an act may be purely good. This occurs when the
act is a value realization that also violates no humane purpose, for
example, breathing fresh air, some pleasant exercise, and endless
others in appropriate contexts. Most acts probably are mixed. They
involve some harm to oneself or others as well as good. But where
the good is great, such as passing an excellent piece of legislation,
the wear and tear of the effort and the toes stepped on and noses
pinched dim out, and one tends to appraise the act as sheer good.
It is not, of course. But many ordinary acts are just such mixtures as
this of good and evil, falling short of requirements by some amount
yet coming so close that the distance is considered negligible and
written off.

It may be objected that no human act can be purely good. Each
such act is the work of a limited creature and limitation is evil.
Evil is inescapable in finite man. Should we agree that limitation is

evil, this argument would be decisive. But there seems no reason to agree to this at least from the human point of view. Indeed, one might argue that limitation is a virtue. Each sentence one writes well has definite or limited meaning. If it did not, it would be unintelligible. Limitation is the basis of realization. No one can realize everything in every which way, only something in some definite way. Thus, there seems no good reason to accept the view that for the human being limitation is evil, and this disposes of the argument. It remains the case, however, that acts purely good are not the most conspicuous type of human act. They are the minor deeds or the rarities. The gruesome reportorial mixture of evil and good served up for breakfast each morning by our newspapers, radio, and television as news of the world may be a travesty on the value quality of our culture. But the mixture could hardly be replaced in volume, not to mention piquancy, by daily acts purely humane doing great good and offending no legitimate purpose.

Culture

We have noted that, besides being governed by a differentiating telic pattern, the activity of a domain may serve numerous additional ends and have numerous additional values or disvalues. Politics may influence science, art, education, family life as these may influence politics or each other. This interlocking of domains and their interdependence suggest the possibility of a concrete systematic interconnection wherein domains unite to form a complex whole. Such a constellation of activities, conceived as operating within a geographic area, a province, a nation, a world, might properly be called a culture, since it constitutes the way that human life there is cultivated and developed and grown.[5]

This concept of a culture as a constellation of domains may suggest that a culture is a secondary and derived phenomenon, the product of an amalgam. But the reverse might be cogently argued.

---

[5] Cf. Clyde Kluckhohn, "Anthropology," in *What Is Science?*, ed. by James R. Newman (New York: Simon and Schuster Co., 1955), pp. 338, 343: "Each culture consists of a linked series of man-made patterns and constitutes a selective way of thinking, feeling, and reacting . . . the essence of this selectivity resides in the value system. Man is not only the tool-using animal; he is also the valuing animal, constantly making judgments of 'better' and 'worse' and behaving in terms of preferences that are by no means altogether reducible to biological needs and to the immediate situation."

Thus even where a major activity of a domain is changing a raw natural object into a cultural object, as in mining, flood control, and the like, this changing ordinarily occurs in a cultural setting and according to certain cultural presuppositions. Culture, it might be said, is the concrete phenomenon; domains, as operating within it, are abstractions from culture. Certainly a domain in the concrete, no more than a human individual, is self-complete or independent of the social environment; and just as "the physiological and biochemical systems (of the human individual) are different at different altitudes,"[6] so a domain is different according to its ambient culture. This is not to deny that domains have their own nature with common properties. Indeed, we have been portraying and emphasizing just this nature with its common properties, such as telic structure and telic requirements, and we shall return to this later. But such common properties are, in the mathematical sense, variables capable of many specific "values," and these specific values are various and not altogether independent of the social environment.

However, we would want to argue also that the domain values are not wholly determined environmentally. History gives us a portrait of the great varieties of human culture, and it sometimes seems to suggest that domains and individuals in their concrete being are by-products of larger cultural forces. Such determinism is a great oversimplification of a complex matter. The individual, for example, is not a culture phonograph playing back some antecedently fixed social set-up in mechanical fashion. He is in a small way a maker of the diversity of his culture. A social environment, it is true, allows him only a finite set of possibilities: in ancient Greece with its musical resources it would not have been possible for Beethoven to have written what we now call the music of Beethoven. Also, the individual being deeply impregnated from childhood by the antecedent slant of his social environment is motivated unconsciously by a vast variety of its value tendencies. So far, there is social determinism. Nevertheless, at no level, is the individual a mere wax tablet or reproducing disc. He is an environment-receiver but also an environment-transformer, passing

[6] Carlos Monge, "Biological Basis of Human Behavior," in *Anthropology Today*, ed. by A. L. Kroeber (Chicago: University of Chicago Press, 1953), p. 132.

53457

its influence through the medium of his temperament, desires, and imagination, and in his actions giving some personal accent to his cultural presuppositions. His actions as personally colored and similar actions by groups of individuals are the architect of social change and vital in determining the final historical contour of a domain and a culture. Accident, natural favor, mishap, fortune generally also may play a part, conditioning and limiting a domain activity. But even combined with the cultural setting these fortuitous elements do not give the activity in a domain its full particularized shape, which always involves the transforming power of individual human beings and groups with their unique properties.

Once this power in individuals and groups is recognized, and the particularized historic form of a domain in the concrete is seen to be a joint product of agent action and environmental conditions, the concept of a culture as a complex whole of domains can be seen in its proper light. As a constellation of domains in a geographic area, a culture primarily is neither an antecedent conditioning force nor an afterproduct of individual and group activity. It is rather the *activity itself* as articulating the various domains. The cultural environs of a limited activity may antecedently condition this activity which itself may have many aftereffects in the society. But the culture itself is the inclusive diversity of conditioning and conditioned acts in the stipulated region.

So conceived, a culture can be appropriately assigned certain properties. First, a culture can be said to have a variety of organs (domain institutions) and functions (domain purposes) and just as the organs and functions of the human body may continue, even with changes in the particular material maintaining them, so the organs and functions of a culture may continue with different human individuals and groups, although they will be modified by the diverse capacities and talents of the new individuals and groups. The new individuals and groups *do* make a difference, but it is a difference within organs and functions that, so long as they remain, are ordinarily similar in general aspects. Again, cultures may be said to have diverse over-all configurations. A culture may be dominated by some domain activity to which the other domain activities are handmaidens, for example, by religion, agriculture, seafaring, or "business." It may be austere, pleasure-loving, commercial, military. Like an individual human being, it may have a "personality" with a complex scale of values ordered according to some principle of dominance, balance, or harmony. Indeed, in a limited sense, it might be assigned an "unconscious," namely, an inheritance of values or traditions passed on with modifications from generation to generation, despite upheavals, and controlling its leaders far more than they may be aware it does.

This concept of a culture as an individuated constellation of domains is close to the concept of a society. The chief difference I believe is really one of emphasis. A culture refers more directly to the activities which people of a geographic area maintain, a society to the people themselves and their institutional set-up. There are other commonly asserted differences. For example, a society is sometimes said to have many cultures (a polyglot society), or, to be part of a culture, as the United States of America is said to be part of modern Western culture. Still, for every society there *is* a culture—namely, the system of domain activities in it—and this culture, as in the polyglot society, may be said to be composed of many cultures, or like the U.S.A., be a part of a larger culture. In respect to extension, "society" and "culture" hence may be said to overlap or be interchangeable.

However, whether the terms are used as interchangeable or not, enough has been said I believe to indicate that both a culture and a society have a general nature and a specific configuration, and are open to general scientific study. Of course, anthropology and sociology exist. But I mean here by "scientific" much more than a conventional imitation of natural science. Like the domains (and individuals and situations) composing them, a society or culture is a complex of goal-oriented activities that settle into some sort of configured pattern defined by telic peculiarities. It is therefore open to the same kind of "objective" structural analysis that a domain is. Moreover, not only can a society or culture be viewed as having certain common or universal components,[7] but it may be conceived as having certain functional prerequisites.

A promising social analysis is a tentative formulation of the functional

---

[7] Bronislaw Malinowski, *The Dynamics of Cultural Change* (New Haven, Conn.: Yale University Press, 1945), pp. 42 ff. (Chap. IV), lists as common components of culture (1) economic organization, (2) system of norms, (3) law or organization of force, (4) mechanisms and agencies of education, (5) system of knowledge, (6) religion, (7) arts.

prerequisites of a society. Functional prerequisites refer broadly to the things that must get done in any society if it is to continue as a going concern, *i.e.*, the generalized conditions necessary for the maintenance of the system concerned. The specific structural arrangements for meeting the functional prerequisites differ, of course, from one society to another and, in the course of time, change in any given society. Thus, all societies must allocate goods and services somehow. A particular society may change from one method, say business enterprise, to another, say a centrally planned economy, without the destruction of the society as a society but merely with a change in its concrete structures.[8]

Such prerequisites or requirements might be conceived to constitute a set of value criteria.[9] However, a scientific analysis of society of this sort would remain ambiguous, and indeed incapable of turning its "functional prerequisites" into "value criteria," until it developed a concept of value on which value criteria and requirements might be based. When this was done, and the concept of value was applied to culture and society portraying the value possibilities there, a type of science quite different from a natural science would take shape, and this type of science is obviously as applicable to domains as it would become applicable to society or culture.

---

[8] D. Aberle *et al.*, "The Functional Prerequisites of a Society," *Ethics*, Vol. LX, No. 2 (1950), quoted by Clyde Kluckhohn, "Universal Categories of Culture," in Kroeber, *Anthropology Today*, p. 513.

[9] Cf. B. J. Diggs, "Ethics and Experimental Theories of Motivation and Learning," *Ethics*, Vol. LXVII, No. 2 (1957), p. 108.

VII
SCIENCES

Sense

It has frequently been argued that there is a clear and irreducible difference between statements of fact and statements of value. To say "X is sodium" and "X is good" is to make statements different not merely in detail but in kind. To attempt to reduce the second type of statement to the first is to commit the "naturalistic fallacy." To attempt to reduce the first type to the second is to commit the "idealistic fallacy." In the present discussion, I shall not argue that in some sense all of this is not true, although plainly, according to our argument up to this point, a value is a fact of a certain kind and "fact" in the above distinction is therefore being used in a limited sense. But let us grant that this conventional dichotomy between factual and value statements represents a kind of truth. What does it involve?

Those who insist most strongly on the dichotomy often take the following view. "X is sodium" or any factual statement describes what is or appears to be an "objective" ingredient or feature of the world. "X is good" or any value statement describes nothing "objective," but merely expresses an emotion, appraisal, approval, imperative, preference, persuasion, liking, wish, in short, a subjective attitude. This is the emotive theory of value statements previously discussed, and the question we wish to ask now about it is: how far does the emotive theory take us in the theory of statements? The answer I think is: not very far. The emotive theory gives us a highly simplified version of the difference between factual and value statements even in the above sense and needs replacement by a more concrete view.

For example, in a concrete context, notice that a statement such as "X is sodium" may possess an emotive, persuasive, imperative element. A person may say: "With this stuff I am all set," but another may remark: "No, I think not. You are mistaken about this stuff. It (X) is sodium." In such a context, "It (X) is sodium" is, or purports to be, a factual statement. Yet obviously it also contains an interdiction or warning, that is, an emotive element. The point of the example is not that in concrete situations factual statements are emotive statements. Such statements remain factual even with an emotive element included. The point is that so-called pure factual statements are usually highly abstract. A factual statement (in the present limited sense of "factual" to be understood throughout this discussion) becomes pure by ignoring, suppressing, or abstracting from emotive and a number of other elements. One of these elements is the purpose context in which these statements usually occur. Generally speaking, in concrete situations, factual statements are purposeful, not purposeless. Even in natural science, indeed especially in natural science, they arise within some ongoing telic enterprise. They have therefore a value element in them, namely, a value for the ongoing enterprise, and only by suppressing this element, or by considering the statements in abstraction from it, do they become purely factual and seem to have no value aspect.

A second point regarding the emotive interpretation of factual and value statements is even more important than this first, namely, there are two perfectly legitimate meanings of "sense" and not merely one or the factual meaning, as the emotive philosophers assume. For example, a person may agree with another who says: "The earth is a planet" yet retort: "So what? What sense does that make? We were talking about sodium, not planets." In this situation, you have a statement ("The earth is a planet") with admitted factual sense being questioned as to whether it has any sense. Why? Clearly because the statement seems to have no relevance to the ongoing purposive concern in the situation into which it has been injected. Often, the essence of nonsense is to introduce a statement perfectly meaningful factually into a purposive context in which it is incongruous, or irrelevant. You may say "Shake-speare is a poet" while a person is planning a course of action, and you may be told: "talk sense, cut out this nonsense." I submit that in concrete "life" situations, this second meaning of sense and nonsense is just as correct as the factual meaning and often more important. If this is the case, as I believe it is, it would seem neces-sary to give full recognition to this meaning in a philosophical theory of human situations, wherever it is useful to do so.

Let us now return to the statement: "X is good." When emotive theorists argue that "good" here corresponds to nothing objective I think we may agree, if by "objective" is meant something that has sense in their (very limited) factual meaning of the term. "Good," I believe, is not like color, weight, mass: a quality that can be found in a purely mechanical context in abstraction from all pur-pose. Ascribed to items in such a merely mechanical context,[1] "good" makes no sense and is necessarily a vacuous or nonsense predicate. But human activity in its usual concrete form, including the activity of the scientist, does not occur in such a merely mechanical context. It has purpose or intent, and when you view human activity in this way, for example, view Y as intent on X, the case is very different. Then "good" has a clear-cut "objective" meaning. When Y says, "X is good," he means that X (say, a paint-ing) exhibits certain intrinsic (terminal) or instrumental fulfillments he has required of it in his situation. That is, he means something about X in relation to his intent or purpose. And this meaning of "X is good" is "objective" or publicly verifiable. It can be discovered to be true or false, in Y's sense, or even in another perhaps more correct sense, by all equally who know X and Y, and specifically know the terminal or instrumental qualities of X and the re-quirements of the purpose of Y, or more correct telic requirements. (On the meaning of "objective" see Chap. IV, Sec. 1.)

The inadequacy of the emotive theory here, I think, is a conse-quence of blandly assuming, on the prestige of natural science, that the abstract causal or mechanical way of looking at X is the only publicly correct way, and that the abstract factual meaning of sense and objectivity in natural science is the only legitimate

---

[1] Cf. Rene Descartes, *Meditations on First Philosophy*, Meditation VI, in *The Philosophical Works of Descartes*, trans. by E. S. Haldane and G. R. T. Ross (Cambridge: Cambridge University Press, 1911), Vol. I, p. 195.

meaning of sense and objectivity. Under this assumption, as I have said, "good" has no objective meaning, and, if it has any meaning at all, as it obviously has, this meaning must be subjective. The appropriate corrective of the emotive theory here, as I have suggested, is to take a less abstract view, and in particular to recognize what human activity, including activity in the natural sciences, fully is. When this is done, it becomes clear, I think, that purpose is as central and fundamental in human activity as mechanism and causality in nature, and that purpose permits a perfectly legitimate meaning of "sense" to be ascribed to human value statements and activities, and a perfectly legitimate parallel meaning of "objective" to be ascribed to human values, additional to the meaning of "sense" and "objective" assigned to factual statements and facts on the assumptions of the emotive theory.

I wish now to indicate a weighty conclusion that seems to me to follow from these elementary observations.

Modern causal science, studying quantitatively the functional or dependence relations between "factual" variables in nature, has been with us for a long time. It was established by Copernicus, Galileo, and others, and its most illustrious exemplification is modern physical theory. Also, for some time, indeed dating back at least to Thomas Hobbes (1588-1679), modern psychology and social science have sought to imitate the physical model, and in recent times, particularly, have succeeded in turning out enormous quantities of causally descriptive statements about human behavior, since there are causal relations in human and social life, as in the physical world. Beginning with the rise in the nineteenth century of biology to major scientific status, however, there has been a growing uneasiness about this trend, and I believe this feeling has been entirely justified. Moving up the scale from physical to human beings, the telic factor in fact becomes increasingly basic and prominent, and inquiry that is committed in its premises to abstract from or suppress it, or to treat it merely as one more causal factor, is committed to overlooking something unique in the nature of existence. Moreover, if what we have just been saying is correct, this unique factor, the telic, is capable of as "objective" and sense-full a treatment as the mechanical or causal factor to which, up to this time, such enormous industry has been devoted. Indeed, considering only the variety of purposive domains in human existence, and not mentioning the complexity of a great many of them, politics, art, science, and more, each of which is itself an enormous field for cognitive exploration, this telic factor opens up the possibility of a variety of new sciences that in number and even more in importance could easily become the equal of the large variety of causal sciences already with us.

This possibility raises innumerable problems of detail that cannot be considered in a single chapter on the subject. But the basic general questions raised fall well within the scope of our inquiry, and call for careful comment. They concern the subject matter, component parts, method, and goals of these so-called new sciences.

Obviously, the primary subject matter of these sciences would be the purpose structure of human activity. Limiting our discussion at first to domains, which will amply illustrate the general character of these sciences, even when they are extended to complex areas such as a society or a culture, let me introduce a few distinctions. In the study of any domain or field of human activity, one can distinguish a theoretical inquiry, the practice entailed by this inquiry, and the practice itself. For example, regarding medicine as a domain or field of human activity directed toward preventing and/or curing disease and establishing health, one can distinguish theories of medicine: somatic, psychosomatic, psychotherapeutic, and the like; the practice that each theory involves; and the actual practicing of medicine. And a similar set of distinctions I think can be applied to any value domain. However, only the first two components, the theory and its implied practice, would be internal constituents of a value science. Actual practice is more than science, being an art in a sense to be specified later.

Theory

Turning to theory first, what would this involve in a value science?

The first thing would be an investigation of the telic structure distinguishing a field of human activity. The pattern studied may be in any field or subfield, for example, natural science or electronics, fine art or sculpture. In this chapter, I have already suggested in a very incomplete form a conception of the telic pattern of natural science. Stated more fully, the pattern of its activity is one in which abstraction is made of all purpose except the scientist's own purpose of finding and describing the causal variables and the systems of causal variables in areas of nature—the "facts" in the narrow sense—and predicting and controlling events, so far as possible, on the basis of these causal findings. Discovery, description, prediction, control in regard to areas of nature: these aims would be found in the natural science telic pattern. Of course, this is a very cryptic and rough outline of the telic structure or goals of this field of human activity. All the key terms we have used call for considerable refinement. "Variable," "factual," "system," "nature," "causal" need fuller definition, as do the relevant meanings of "discovery," "description," "prediction," "control." Indeed, to clarify all such parts of the purpose structure of natural science would be exactly the first major task here of the theoretical side of value science. And to perform a similar task in regard to all distinguishable fields of human effort: fine art, economics, politics, and the others, would be the first major task in developing the theoretical side of the new value sciences.

It should be fairly evident from this illustration of natural science that constructing satisfactory descriptions of the telic patterns of any of these fields or domains is a very large undertaking. It would require great factual knowledge of each field, an equal understanding of the purposes actually operating throughout the field, a well-grounded discernment of each domain's value possibilities, a knowledge of the important discussions of these matters, and a skillful use of all of this information. Under present conditions, some of these requirements can be met fairly well in some fields, for example, in theory of science.[2] But even the best results at present are hardly more than pioneering approximations on the theoretical level, since the problem of the new sciences has not heretofore been stated in its full range and the kinds of information useful for answering its questions have not been developed in high degree. At the same time, however, regarding the domains or fields themselves, the theoretical problem is *in principle* solvable. Fine art is not natural science, and natural science is not politics. They all have distinctive aims along with any overlapping aims, and this is common knowledge widely recognized. In principle, therefore,

---

[2] Norman Campbell, *What Is Science?* (New York: Dover Publications, Inc., 1952); *Readings in the Philosophy of Science*, ed. by H. Feigl and M. Brodbeck (New York: Appleton-Century-Crofts, Inc., 1953); and *What Is Science?*, ed. by J. R. Newman (New York: Simon and Schuster Co., 1955), Bibliography, pp. 437 ff., supply a number of examples of different essays in the theory of science.

it should be possible to disentangle a distinctive telic pattern for each domain, and thereby to determine the key value principle—the purpose structure—that gives items special sense and significance as items in each field.[3]

As to the method to be used on the primary subject matter, and in other parts of a value science, it would be the same in general character as used in any science. Besides the accumulation of data such as the information mentioned in the preceding paragraph, the method would consist of a skillful use of this data in the invention of hypotheses, elaboration and unification of hypotheses, and systematization of subordinate hypotheses and ideas under a central theoretical projection. The main generic differences between a value science and any other type of science would be subject matter, and, as a consequence, the different kinds of tools, physical and mathematical, useful for accumulating data and testing hypotheses. Also, while the method would naturally take its point of departure from divisions of human activities bearing conventional names (art, politics, and the like), as early natural science accepted the conventional divisions of nature, the method might be expected to lead to some recasting of these divisions and to staking out novel domains, since its business is not the clarification of tradition but the delineation of differential telic structures in their actual operation.

In such broad respects, then, the method of a value science would parallel exactly the general scientific method of theoretical inquiry, and this methodological similarity, despite differences in specific subject matter and techniques, is one reason for using the term "science" or "sciences" for the proposed types of inquiry.

Two topics already discussed in the preceding chapter are relevant at this point.

In the last chapter we noted that a domain usually has implications for others, politics for fine art, science for politics, and so forth. Hence, while the focus of a theoretical investigation should be on the differentiating telic structure of a domain, and its inner

[3] D. W. Gotshalk, *Art and the Social Order* (Chicago: University of Chicago Press, 1947, 1951; New York: Dover Publications, Inc., 1962), Chapters I-III illustrate an effort to describe the distinctive telic structure of fine art as a human activity. For a very different type of illustration, cf. Peter Winch, *The Idea of a Social Science* (London: Routledge & Kegan Paul; New York: Humanities Press, Inc., 1958).

requirements, this investigation in full scope would also include the connections with other domains and the variety of purposes and values that accrue to a domain from these connections. No domain appears to be monadic or sealed off; hence, no scientific investigation of it should be similarly confined. Second, we also noted, the terms in which the differentiating telic structure of a domain should be described, should be sufficiently general to include all the diversity and variety of items of the region. The persistent aim should be concrete unity of view. Among other things, this means that a theoretic investigation should seek a logical simplification of its field so that two or more items in it that may seem contradictory or incompatible under existing concepts will be fitted into a more general unifying conception.[4] This logical simplification must be complete in the sense that the fundamental variables are general enough that they can efficiently encompass all of the distinctive variety of the domain.

Besides these points several others come immediately to mind as important in supplementing the discussion of subject matter and method in this section.

(1) From earliest modern times, as we have observed, most proposals for a science of human values, sometimes called a science of human nature, have been modeled on physics. Hobbes based his proposal mainly on his understanding of Galileo's physics. Hume's suggestion of a science of human nature on the Newtonian model—impressions corresponding to Newtonian corpuscles, laws of association to Newtonian laws of motion and gravitation—is also in the same tradition, as are numerous other proposals. Much current thinking and practice in psychology and the other human and social sciences is in similar vein,[5] sometimes not only copying sedulously physical methods but insisting on what is taken to be the physical outlook as the essence of "science."

While this is far from our own view, it is perfectly consistent

---

[4] Cf. Horace S. Fries, "Logical Simplicity: A Challenge to Philosophy and to Social Inquiry," *Phil. of Science,* Vol. 17, No. 3 (July, 1950), p. 217, *passim.*

[5] Cf. R. S. Hartman, "The Moral Situation: A Field Theory of Ethics," *Jour. Phil.* (May, 1948), p. 292, and "Is a Science of Ethics Possible?," *Phil. of Science,* Vol. 17, No. 3 (July, 1950), pp. 238 ff.; Charles Morris, "Axiology as the Science of Preferential Behavior," in *Value: A Cooperative Inquiry,* ed. by Ray Lepley (New York: Columbia University Press, 1949), pp. 211 ff.

with our view to believe that the physical and natural sciences have a great and proper role to play in the study of human behavior. To extend their procedure and outlook into the human field, so far as possible, is certainly a legitimate development. Human beings and social complexes are physical agencies and exhibit causal uniformities, and even to treat the telic factor as a cause, for example, to list the number of times a telic factor, such as self-control or self-indulgence, activates a set of individuals in a group, or is praised or dispraised by them,[6] is to accumulate information potentially useful, although the question would remain: useful for what?

However, as I have said, our own proposal is not to extend natural science in this way. Despite the opinion of many severe critics of science, typified by romantics from Schopenhauer to Bergson, and despite the creed of many current scientists, who would limit science to mechanistic natural science, our view is that natural science is not science, but only one form of it, and that science properly is any systematic theoretic inquiry into an empirically accessible field governed by certain aims: "objectivity," accuracy, comprehensiveness, among them. Our proposal is to extend this type of inquiry to the telic factor in its distinctive nature, namely, as a principle of evaluation and the ruling action principle of domains and fields of value. The conception of science as limited to natural science has been a dogma of great strength in modern times, and been particularly constricting in recent times in the human and social fields. "As things stand today," Perry writes, "the (human and) social sciences are more in need of emancipating themselves from the bigotry of natural science than of adopting its method."[7]

(2) Some might question whether the kind of knowledge gathered in a value inquiry could ever properly be called empirical, the subject matter being what it is. This subject matter is different from that of the usual so-called empirical sciences since the differentiating telic pattern in a value field contains the requirements

---

[6] Cf. Charles Morris and Lyle V. Jones, "Value Scales and Dimensions," *Jour. of Abnormal and Social Psychology,* Vol. 51, No. 3 (Nov., 1955), pp. 523 ff. As Morris says ("Axiology as the Science of Preferential Behavior," in Lepley, *Value: A Cooperating Inquiry,* p. 220): The laws of preferential behavior "would tell us who prefers what under what conditions."

[7] R. B. Perry, *Realms of Value* (Cambridge: Harvard University Press, 1954), p. 174.

of what *ought* to operate, not necessarily what is actually operating. Knowledge of the "ought" and "good" is *a priori* and not empirical.[8] However, this view is plausible because these philosophers limit experience to sense-data observation. On this, a knowledge of "ought" and "good" is indeed *a priori* at least in the sense of being nonempirical. However, we have already found difficulties in this sense-data concept of experience.[9] Besides, the term "experience" is commonly given, and for a long time has had a much more usual and less technical meaning, according to which we say that experience has shown in countless instances what government, or science, or technology in competent hands can achieve, and therefore what we ought to demand that it achieve. On this meaning, knowledge of well-grounded value possibilities and requirements clearly is obtainable by experience, and a hypothesis about the purpose structure of a region that includes these possibilities and requirements can be developed in empirical terms.

Furthermore, although the full development of knowledge on this basis is a monumental undertaking, and the best that we can now hope for is tentative approximations needing continuous revision, it is far from true that we have nothing at all to start with. A primitive differentiation of domains is very long-standing. That government is not poetry or landscape painting is kindergarten knowledge. Nor are the value possibilities of numerous domains altogether obscure. Quite the contrary. In the field of ethical action, for example, a great many value possibilities, the so-called virtues, which in some form or other are requirements or strong candidates for requirements of ethical action, are widely known and long practiced. "Hospitality, care of children, fidelity, a certain respect for life and liberty—in short all the major virtues have been practised, as we should say conscientiously, by every people at every time, imperfectly, to be sure, but very manifestly."[10] Indeed, ethical investigation has an enormous backlog of empirical information

[8] C. D. Broad, *Five Types of Ethical Theory* (London: Routledge & Kegan Paul, Ltd., 1930, 1950), pp. 104 ff., *passim;* C. I. Lewis, *An Analysis of Knowledge and Valuation* (La Salle, Ill.: Open Court Publishing Co., 1946), pp. 378 ff., *passim.* For contrast, cf. Kurt Baier, *The Moral Point of View* (Ithaca, N.Y.: Cornell University Press, 1958), Chap. II.

[9] Pp. 14-15.

[10] John Laird, *The Idea of Value* (Cambridge: Cambridge University Press, 1929), p. 233.

to deal with critically and to proceed upon, in developing a more precise and inclusive concept of the authentic and pertinent value possibilities and the differentiating telic structure in its area.

We can sum up this section by saying that the theoretic component of a human value science would be a theory of the telic structure of a human activity, and, in the case of a domain, a theory of the telic pattern of a domain. This theory would be based primarily on the method of hypothesis and experience above described, or more fully, on the method of rational experience described in the second chapter. These domain inquiries might well culminate in an interconnecting of the various domain patterns with some more fundamental one, for example, at one end with the telic pattern of a culture, at the other with the telic structure of human nature.

Besides its telic form, there is another side to human activity. Activity means doing or practice in the broadest sense. A theory of the structure of a domain activity, setting out possibilities and requirements, would therefore have important implications for practice.

Practice

To begin with an illustration: suppose it were possible, in the approximate and tentative manner already mentioned, to describe the distinctive purpose structure of a fine art, to outline the value possibilities in it, and to provide thereby a set of value requirements for productions seeking to excel in this art or to have sense and significance in it.

Obviously, for practice this would imply translating the value requirements into a set of procedures and adapting the procedures to the actual conditions under which they would be applied. In a certain type of work, fresco, for example, this would involve knowledge of the necessary instruments of the artist, of the required training, and of the physical and social circumstances most favorable to realization in the art. With this knowledge at hand, the proper procedures could be set up, and efforts made to show how to adapt them to actual conditions. It may be asked: but is this not just what has always been done in any art? Has it not always been based on a knowledge of instruments, on technical training, and adaptation to actual conditions? The answer is that this has indeed been the case. The difference between the traditional and our proposed *practica* lies in the scientific background that the new practice would substitute for the traditional rule-of-thumb understanding of the value possibilities in the field. Instead of vague and disorganized goals or the narrow purposes so often accepted in the past, and in the present also, as adequate ends, the education in practice and the consequent practice would be grounded on the best systematic insights into the value possibilities of the field, and these insights would color and guide the knowledge of instruments, the technical training, and the production process in all its phases.

I call knowledge of instruments, of procedures, of circumstances, practical, because it points to modes of practice. But in a sense such knowledge is theoretical. It does not tell the artist the specific things he must do in a given case. It maps a generic course of action. Thus, to change the example, the laboratory practices in physics to be used to verify an as yet unknown theory can hardly all be specified in advance, nor can all the engineering instruments and procedures to be used in building an as yet unplanned tunnel or highway. The situation is generally parallel to that in medicine. Practical training in medicine, as in internship, does not show the fledgling doctor all that he must do in every specific case. It shows him merely what good medical understanding and the purposes of medicine imply at present for instances of a certain type of case. It gives the doctor merely a general outline of procedures. The application of these generic procedures to new instances is up to the doctor who must judge what is relevant and irrelevant and carry through the selected procedures with sensitivity to the demands of the case before him.

As to handling the particular case itself, as I have said, this is in a sense outside value science as it is outside medical science. It involves what is sometimes called "art," or, more accurately, the skillful application of knowledge to a specific situation so as to realize the purpose of the activity there. This application includes more than a theory and a practical program. Indeed, an insensitive "mechanical" application of even an infallible theory and set of practical procedures would be no guarantee of success at all in practice. Moreover, as I think we have made clear, no value science in its theory or implied practice is likely to be infallible. In specific cases, correction of the current theory and practice may be necessary to achieve the domain end in view, just as doctors of great insight and skill are often forced to go beyond current medical theory and practice to handle certain cases, thereby enriching frequently the theory and practice in their field.

Nevertheless, it remains true that with a background of science, theoretical and practical, with a systematic illumination of genuine value possibilities translated into procedures generically adapted to actual conditions, individuals in medicine, fine art, and other regions of value activity are likely on the whole to decide and act better than others without this background, and the exceptions we have just cited are not of persons without this background but of trained personnel with gifts enabling them to enrich it with new insights. In this respect, that is, as generally handled better by the scientifically trained, the particular case is very much within the field of value science, although in another respect it is beyond mere science, and requires talent, even genius, of another kind.

Applied to values and particularly to "humanist" activities, the term "science" often arouses the strongest kind of emotional opposition. Is there no place in human life for individual freedom, private preference, impulse, temperament? Must all human beings be machined into standard patterns of activity? *Brave New World* and *1984* are popular symbols of this protest, and one great appeal of emotive theories and of certain types of existentialism and subjectivism in recent years has been that they seem to assign a secure place in the humanist realm to individual freedom and private preference. I think it would be unfortunate if a conception of the value sciences should fail to do this. However, the important consideration is that the individual and the private be given not merely a secure place but an appropriate place. And it is a question whether recent doctrines such as the emotive theory do this.

A domain of human activity obviously involves much more than any one person's private impulses or individual freedom. It involves a multitude of persons and situations. Now, individual inclination and preference may be in harmony with a domain pattern. So far, there can be no argument. But where they are not, their exercise, as authoritative in the domain, seems clearly open to question. Let us suppose that the theory application in a given situation is the appreciation of two artistic forms, a Giotto and a Rubens, and further that both are good artistic forms in a sense determinable within a value science, namely, both forms fulfill the purpose or role of form in fine art to a high degree. The character of good here is not a matter of private inclination and preference. It is a question of knowing the role of form in fine art, of inspecting the two works, and of seeing the congruence of the forms with the demands on form in fine art. You may, however, personally prefer one form to the other, the Giotto to the Rubens, or vice versa. This is surely legitimate. But your individual preference for one form, if that is all that is involved, does not detract in the least from the artistic value of the other form. All that it does is to give one artistically good form more private value to you than the other form that is also good artistically.

This point, that individual inclination and preference are one basis of value only, and a basis of private not of public value, may be clarified by another illustration. Suppose a person is looking at a universally admitted botched artistic form and says that he likes it. Another person says: "You mean that it is a good artistic form?" The first person replies: "Yes, of course. Good is what I like." This position seems to be exactly what some emotive theories would have us believe. Yet the position clearly has its ironies. The artistic form in question is botched, all parties agree. Moreover, the liking of the first person does not alter this fact in the sense in which it is admitted. What, then, does it do? What is its significance? It indicates, I believe, merely that the first person in this case is not intent on good artistic form but upon something else, for instance, enjoying the stimulations of a botched form. That is, his liking here is irrelevant and meaningless as a determiner of good form and merely indicates a private enjoyment value additional to the value or lack of value of the form as a good artistic achievement.

One conspicuous characteristic of modern times has been the attempt to deny universal or public value, or to reduce it to private value, or to subordinate it to private inclination and preference. This is one form of the malady of egoistic individualism characteristic of many phases of postmedieval Western civilization. The relief from it, I think, is to see that the two types of value, private and public, are genuine and distinct, and are correlated with different aspects of man's purposive activity, for example, subjective enjoyment and "objective" achievement. Such a view does not make private value any less important and precious. It merely keeps it private. At the same time, it clears the ground for a genuine, "objective," and public science of value or a set of sciences, that need not deny the importance of the subjective and individual when they are assigned their appropriate place.

This last statement, and indeed all of the above discussion of the place of individual inclination and talent in human activity, raises the problem of the general aims or goals of the value sciences on the "practical" side, as well as in their theoretical development.

Goals

The natural science outlook in the field of values, the discovery of causal laws telling what type of human being will do what and prefer what under what conditions, has had a curious development on the practical side. As some progress has been made, motivational research has been taken up by business and has suggested techniques of advertising and salesmanship. The "practical" goal has been manipulation, or by various devices, getting the horse not only to the trough but also to drinking. This is the temptation on the practical side of other recent human "sciences": operations research, game theory, decision-making inquiry, social management, social engineering, namely, to become techniques of commercial exploitation.

In contrast to this aim, the goals of the value sciences as here conceived might be described in this way: in theory construction, the goal is to clarify the distinctive telic patterns of human activities, their principles of good and evil, and the requirements that these patterns impose, their principles of right and wrong. On the practical side, the aim of the value sciences is to portray what is implied by the theory for practice to realize the good and the right. More particularly, the goal of the *practica* is to help train competence in a value area. Just as proper instruction in a sport, say golf, aims primarily not at manipulating the pupil for the instructor's private gain, but at making the pupil into an abler golfer, so the practical side of a value science would be concerned primarily with developing through knowledge more able activity or improved conditions in a value domain. The goal would be enhanced value stature in individual or group attainment.

This conception approaches the idea of manipulation in its unsavory sense where a domain has human beings for objects, for example, in medicine, education, government. Indeed, practical activity at its best here does require skill in handling people, and a kind of social "engineering" or social "management." But an important distinction should be drawn. This is between the use of knowledge to exploit people primarily for the exploiter's ends, and the use of knowledge primarily to realize the domain purpose (health, good education, good government) in the object. Both are social "engineering" in the sense of handling people on the basis of knowledge to get certain results. But the difference is between trickery for the advantage of the trickster, and the development of people for ends advantageous to them as members of the domain. It is this last, according to our view, that is in practice the goal of the knowledge furnished by a value science in domains having human beings as objects.

This concept of goals is intended to apply to all types of domains, "negative" as well as "positive." War and murder are domains, as much as medicine and education. The study of their purpose structure and the implications of this study for practice would be among the value sciences, when it was undertaken from the standpoint of the good rather than from a narrowly technical interest in the execution of their purpose. Some differences in detail of theory and practice would naturally appear in the science of negative domains. Thus, the theoretical scrutiny of these domains would delineate the purpose structure as involving possibilities of value destruction in excess of the possibilities of value achievement. Consequently, the *practica* of the value science, devoted to realizing in action the good and the right, would emphasize here techniques to prevent the operation of this purpose structure, or to diminish its baleful effects. Indeed, only in this way would the value science itself conform to the demands of the good made in its own field of activity. Apart from this, however, the goal of value science, in all domains, would be the same twofold aim: knowledge of the unique purpose structure and its requirements, and such guidance as to realize in practice the good and the right, on the basis of the theoretic knowledge.

Some who advocate the development of a science of value urge pooling of our knowledge in the natural sciences, especially biology and psychology, for the purpose.[11] This is a most acceptable suggestion in line with our whole argument. But the assump-

---

[11] Cf. Abraham Edel, *Ethical Judgment: The Use of Science in Ethics* (Glencoe, Ill.: The Free Press, 1955).

tion sometimes is also made that such pooling will solve the problems of value science. This seems to me completely mistaken. As I have suggested, in value studies we *do* need knowledge based upon the natural science approach, particularly about the causal processes of human beings. No conception of human purpose valuable for practice can ignore causal factors, not merely because the purpose of a human activity (say, medicine) must be conceived in terms of them (e.g., in terms of the way the body works) but mainly because the purpose must be executed by means of them (e.g., of these "workings" redirected) and therefore in harmony with them, to be effective. Still a conception of what ought to be executed is not disclosed merely by a knowledge of what is going on. Physics and chemistry are not medicine. They require an additional perspective. And, generally, all the knowledge in the world about what human beings do do, and what affects them in what manner, is of no avail in determining what they ought to do or what is good for them to do, unless one has a principle of value clarified and tested to grade what they do and what affects them.

A person may complain: why propose a large number of new lines of scientific research when we are already stupified by the massive accumulations of scientific information now in our possession? Also, how can we be sure that your proposed type of scientific inquiry will yield fruitful results?

To this second question, the only answer I fear is that we cannot be sure. In varying degrees all science is a gamble, and this is certainly the case with the proposed human sciences, at least in their practical application. The actions of human beings in so many instances seem hopelessly wild, erratic, irrational. That human purpose might come to submit to rational order in certain areas seems an almost astronomical possibility. Still, something like this could have been said about physical processes before the inception of the natural sciences. Not too long ago, among earlier civilizations, the belief was that "nature" is properly an object for magic, tribal incantation, and superstitious hocus-pocus. Its actions are a result of caprice, not of causes capable of rational description and, in some cases, rational direction. Nevertheless, by a long and painful effort, particularly in postmedieval times, natural processes have been shown to be capable of being described (and in some cases directed) in a rational manner. Why should human purpose remain in so many domains a creature of irrational expression and manipulation if in its various areas it shows itself to have a unique public nature and by analytic treatment can furnish principles for intelligently guiding value activity?

As to the stupefying character of the scientific knowledge already accumulated, this may be true in certain fields; at least it may seem true to an outsider. But knowledge of the telic side of man, particularly systematic theoretic conceptions of the distinctive purpose structures of domain activities and of their unique possibilities for human well-being: this can hardly be said to exist in abundance. To be sure, we know a few things, and in certain areas quite a few things. But there is no area of human activity about which we know so much on the telic side that our knowledge seriously approaches the authority of our physical knowledge. In this circumstance, the proposal to increase this knowledge with the possible consequence of introducing greater rationality into human purpose and public order can hardly be considered at this time unnecessary or unwelcome. Furthermore, the discovery of such rational conceptions might have the advantage of simplifying our vast and growing aggregates of causal knowledge by giving these aggregates more intelligible and unified direction. But probably, if successfully developed, the chief practical advantage of the value sciences would be to furnish foundations for a program to stem the telic irrationalities that have so markedly and tragically disfigured, and still disfigure, human life in the twentieth century.[12] Should the value sciences be developed to this high level in due time, the natural sciences and their applications could no longer be looked upon, even by their partisans, as the one unfailing cornucopia of the good and the only reliable means to the attainment of the good life in modern times.

---

[12] Cf. D. W. Gotshalk, *The Promise of Modern Life* (Yellow Springs, Ohio: Antioch Press, 1958), Chap. IV.

VIII
THE GOOD LIFE

Individuals

So far, our main topics have been the polar components of the value situation, the principle of value, the domains of value, and our knowledge of values. An additional topic of obvious importance is the good life or the life of value, and since this is synoptic in nature, it will enable us to bring together in new focus some of the fundamental implications of our analysis of the other value topics.

Like a domain, the human individual as we have interpreted him has a distinctive *telos*. His multitude of impulses, desires, and drives are differentiated into an individual system by his physical structure, his training, his temperament, and similar factors. This differentiated *telos*, at each of its diverse stages of growth, determines by its range the possibilities of value compatible with the individual's being. Ideally, the good life for the individual would seem to be to realize as he goes along these value possibilities.

Fundamentally, this really means two things. First and obviously, it means a life congenial to the individual's nature. The demands of work and play, education and friends, and of whatever other objects or pursuits give substance to human life, would come within the individual's physical and psychical capabilities, giving them opportunity for full but agreeable exertion. These demands would exist in amount and intensity sufficient to challenge all his powers, but not in a strength that would overwhelm them. There would be a kind of live wholeness or integrity to the individual's existence, in contrast to the existence of the unchallenged or overchallenged, the complacent or the broken individual, which would lack liveness or wholeness of being.

But the good life as above described has a second meaning. It means *realization* of capacities as well as congeniality in the realization. This brings in the domains, for the capabilities of individuals are not merely subjective possessions. They are capacities for work, for friendship, for social undertakings, and usually function within domains with their telic structures and principles of measurement. On this side, the good life or the life really valuable would involve meeting the requirements of the relevant domains. It would be not only doing something you wanted to do, but doing well something that is good to do. It would mean effectiveness as well as gratification. Indeed, only in this way would the individual genuinely realize innumerable possibilities of his being, which are domain possibilities, and bring into his life a certain depth or richness of value to go with the integrity and wholeness that congeniality would give.

I have said that this concept of the good life is an ideal. It is likely to be realized only in a degree. Some there are who doing what they can do and truly want to do are also doing the world's work in superlative fashion. Owing to an almost amazing constellation of factors, good disposition and good luck not least of them, their activities are both personally congenial and socially effective. But how many people are among these? It is important to note in considering such a question that the above concept of the good life does not limit it to a stereotype: a scholar, a banker, a philosopher, an ascetic. The variety that might have a good life in the above sense is very large, as is the variety that might not. An active temperament leading the sedentary life of a scholar might be very miserable, as well as very obnoxious, while a sedentary person forced by family demands to be a salesman or politician might be distraught and incompetent. No doubt, a good life would involve being active and effective in a number of domains. Also, such lives often would involve many of the same domains, since many interests of many human beings coincide. But the possibility of various kinds would remain: farmer, poet, philosopher, king. In any instance, there would be the same two principles, effectiveness and congeniality, but this would be all of the sameness really needed.

"Happiness" is the term customarily employed to describe the substance of the good life for individuals. It is a pleasing term, tempting to use, but unfortunately it has many meanings. There is the happiness of the healthy bullfrog with his lifelong gestalt of immediate satisfactions, and the happiness of the willfully superstitious. Lately many have known the happiness induced by intellectual tranquillizers who supply sedatives to troubled nerves by artificial cheeriness.[1] People today may be in great trouble, and the medications of the happiness boys may be far better for their troubled souls than other drugs on the market. But to be becalmed on a sea of trouble by such artificial stimulants is not exactly the equivalent of the substance of the good life as we are describing it.

However, "happiness" connotes the sweetness and joy of life, a multitude of agreeable states, small fugitive and very private pleasures as when a very pretty and pleasing young lady friend does one an unexpected favor, as well as the more sustained joys of full-tide private and public accomplishment. All this, as the natural accompaniment of congenial and effective activity, would find place in the good life as here conceived. And as we have just noted, this life would also have the character of being potentially open to individuals of many kinds, as happiness is commonly supposed to be. It would require the realization not necessarily of only grand and "heroic" possibilities, but of such capacities as the individual had in those domains suited to his capacities. Further than this, one might describe the good life as I have suggested elsewhere[2] after the analogy of fine art. As in fine art, it would be the use of skill and personal resources to create an object (here, a life) radiant with immanent values. Very likely, the steady

---

[1] Cf. Norman Vincent Peale, *Stay Alive All Your Life* (Englewood Cliffs, N.J.: Prentice-Hall, Inc., 1957), and also *The Power of Positive Thinking* and *A Guide to Confident Living;* Smiley Blanton, *Love or Perish* (New York: Simon and Schuster Co., 1957); Claude Bristol and Harold Sherman, *TNT, the Power Within You* (Englewood Cliffs, N.J.: Prentice-Hall, Inc., 1957); John A. Schindler, *How to Live 365 Days a Year* (Englewood Cliffs, N.J.: Prentice-Hall, Inc., 1954); Hornell Hart, *Autoconditioning* (Englewood Cliffs, N.J.: Prentice-Hall, Inc., 1956).

[2] D. W. Gotshalk, *Art and the Social Order* (Chicago: University of Chicago Press, 1947, 1951; New York: Dover Publications, Inc., 1962), pp. 215-216.

stream of concentrated intrinsic realizations exhibited in works of art at their best is impossible for any long stretch in the life of an ordinary mortal. But something of the spirit of this realization, and approaches to it, seems possible where congeniality and effectiveness are combined in high degree in a value effort.

Choices

Perhaps some may think that the above is really a concept of the mediocre life, not of the truly valuable life, since it does not necessarily require "heroic" attainment. The answer is that where the capacity range of the individual includes the "truly heroic," then, on the above principles, his life if good would require such attainment. The comparative stature of a life is doubtless a function of the comparative stature of the capacities exercised, but its positive goodness or badness has to do with the realization or nonrealization of the capacities actually possessed by the individual.

It may be objected, however, that our concept does ignore many real difficulties in life. One of these is self-knowledge, or, knowing one's capacities. Individuals are frequently uncertain and often mistaken here, and when they come to know their capacities in a rational way, if they ever do, they have usually made so many mistakes or wrong commitments that the jig is up, or nearly so. Nothing remains except to live out one's errors. In general, congeniality—the deeply congenial—often takes a lifetime to discover. And who knows its limits? May not something that seemed at one time against the grain turn out to be surprisingly congenial? What fits one's needs and powers? This is an endlessly recurring question. And what is effectiveness? What is effectiveness in business, in art, in education, in politics, in family life and neighborly associations? And what is an effective proportion between all of these and similar activities? And how are all of these possible in present circumstances?

Perhaps these objections can be best stated in terms of the kind of choices now open to people. Were the individual born an adult, were everything in his life or at least his domain possibilities and personal potentialities spread clearly before him like patterns of good and evil laid on a table, did the individual know how actual circumstances would develop, had he unlimited time to survey all of these things, and had he "real" choice, the good life as we have described it might be relatively easy to achieve, and a common occurrence. But this is not the way things are. We live in a very imperfect world including among its imperfections the limitations of our stages of growth and of our knowledge of ourselves and our circumstances. At the same time, we often *must* make choices. The urgency of need and action will not permit delay. We may not like our work and may not do it very effectively. But we may have to work to "live," and may know of no better work available. We may not think our friends very perfect, nor our physical surroundings including the weather and architecture of our town or country what we would want ideally. But in our situation we may be "stuck" with them. We may not think totalitarianism nor democracy is a very satisfactory form of government, and we may think that nationalism of any type is an abomination of the first order. But we may have been born and reared under a regime with one or more of these political commitments, and have or know nothing better to which to escape. Such imperfections, such occasions for discontent, are genuine and interminable. Does not our description of the good life ignore them? How is such a good life possible when individuals are faced with choices between these real alternatives?

Such questions raise important problems, but I do not think they raise important objections to our concept (or any concept) of the good life. This concept is an attempt to describe what the life of an individual would be *if* it were good, and, while such a life may be difficult to realize or even impossible fully to realize under present circumstances, this does not prove that, if it were realized, it would not be good. Only if some evidence is brought against this, for example, if the things alleged to be ignored in our concept of the good life were claimed to be good (such as man's limited knowledge and circumscribed choices), as they are not, could reference to them be a refutation of our concept of what is good. In general, a value ideal is a description not of what people do or can now do, but of what the good requires. And while this may not describe the actualities of the situation people are in, that was never its intention, nor its proper purpose.

The above questions, however, do raise important problems about historical conditions and the choices people face. Today, in our stalemated world so full of potential terror, the blackness and blankness of life sometimes take on sizable dimensions. The "sick individual in a sick society" is the cliché frequently applied to the typically sensitive person, and through a type of deranged surrealist mind, articulate people often interpret the aberrations of our society, its strong turn to pleasure, excitement, sports, gambling, busy work, and crime, its overorganized sectors of faceless togetherness, its fragmentation into artistic and intellectual and other cults, its myopic overspecialization. The technological utopian and soul-shocked existentialists, so far as they serve as contemporary spiritual guides, illustrate similarly an inward imbalance at the root of a discordant civilization.

Obviously, so far as all of this is true, it indicates a lack of rational command over the conduct of life, and less obviously, but equally, it indicates a kind of widely diffused value undereducation. A people rationally trained in the value areas would not create such an awry world. However, the existence of such a world, if it does exist, should occasion no great surprise when we realize that, while our "scientific" resources for social mischief are being expanded geometrically, a scientific level in the value side of education is almost totally lacking in our culture. That scientifically grounded value education, even in saturated form, would eliminate all of the evils of human existence is not being suggested. Imperfections in nearly all of the best value realizations are probably ineradicable this side of Utopia. But that a powerful and effective, scientifically grounded value education could eliminate the wayward, self-centered, and provincial orientations disturbing the more dangerous areas of public life today, and that it could give clear principles also for solving the less explosive issues in the other areas, should be evident from the type of "objective," universal, and overarching patterns that we have seen properly govern the domains of human activity.

To this two further comments should be added here: (1) Continuing the point just made and relating it to the actual value choices of people today, these choices might be described as not between black and white but usually between several imperfect alternatives. If this is so, then far from being evidence against our concept of the good, these "facts of life" point up the need, particularly in regard to domains, of more detailed scientific development of this concept. If neither democracy nor totalitarianism is good government, for instance, what is good government, and how can it become an actuality in human living? Genuinely extensive theoretic and practical research on the purpose structure of domains might remove the barrenness of the alternatives that so often confront choice now. Thus, the lesson to be drawn from the ugly and imperfect aspects of the contemporary individual's life would seem to be the urgency, not merely the need, for suitable development of the value sciences.

(2) From what has been said in this and the preceding section, it should be evident that the life of the individual in certain general features is like a domain, a "private" domain. It is a field of activity with a telic structure, and its principle of value, furnishing its standard for judging items, is imbedded in it. Indeed, its principle of value is simply its telic or purpose structure, conceived as developed congenially and effectively. To live in accordance with it is to live at "peace" with oneself. To realize its inherent potentialities in domains where they fit effectively is to live at "peace" with the world. Some people find deepest satisfaction in work and achievement. To contribute something permanently useful to the life of mankind, some music, poetry, political action, philosophy, would be the high watermark of existence. Others find deepest satisfaction in leisure and pleasure, in relief from the day's anxious hubbub and chatter. The extremes are the happy loafer and the anxiety-ridden workhorse. Both are cripples with the central artery of achievement or enjoyment blocked and hardened. Only some combination of enjoyment and achievement, in Kant's phrase "happiness" and virtue, or in ours congeniality and effectiveness, seems to meet the full specifications of the inherent telic structure of the human individual.

One of the crucial conditions of the good life of the individual, as the above objections to our concept make clear, is the social context of his existence. Of this context we might say that it is a complex domain, indeed a complex of domains, and it has its own proper purposes. In the course of the ensuing discussion we shall offer a hypothesis regarding this purpose, so far as it relates to the good life of the individual. But let me preface this with a few words about the way in which the social context is exceptionally relevant to the life of the individual.

Society

To have a good life, to live effectively in a deeply congenial manner, usually requires exertion, good judgment, sustained purpose, considerateness, good temper, and similar traits. But it also requires opportunity. A small prison cell may be a suitable setting for some activities. But it is hardly suitable for the great variety of human activity. Subjective potentialities require objective instrumentalities. A potentiality for statesmanship, commerce, education obviously can become actualized only if certain outer means are available. And while these means often are physical, they are usually controlled by human beings, and are open to individuals only under certain social conditions.

Every human being is born into a social order. This order begins with the family, or at least with the parent-child relation, but it is actually as extensive as the human race. This complex order with its many interior orders provides the setting and chief condition of the individual's existence. Physical circumstances may seem independent of it. Air, sunshine, soil, landscape, storms, the seasons: these may appear to be pure products of nonhuman nature. But the more deeply they affect human life, the more strenuous is the effort to bring them under human dominion. Thus, more and more our physical circumstances are socially modified, and society increasingly supplies the all-encompassing conditions of individual existence. Romantics have dreamed of escaping it. But in a total sense there is no escaping it. Not only is there no place one can go, on earth or elsewhere, independent of society, but for a good segment of the individual's life, such as most of his growing years, he is incompetent to go. For various people at various times a change of local setting may be highly desirable. But this is quite different from a total escape, which would require not only an isolated terrain, but the discarding of all habits and training, including language and learning, since these have been acquired from instruction in a society.

Yet society, besides an inescapable and all-encompassing circumstance, is something itself, a complex of domains with its own form and character. What aim should govern such a complex as the context of the good life of the individual?

Perhaps we can state our answer to this question most easily in terms of one analysis of human nature our argument has prepared us to accept. According to this analysis, the human being has a twofold nature. He is a purposive creature with great inner resources capable of development in many directions, as the great variety of his domains attest. He is also a causal creature with limited causal powers living in a vast physical universe. Employing his causal powers and the tools he has invented, and trying where he can to bend physical nature to his uses, he still suffers innumerable reverses, hunger, illness, death, many more. Almost completely confined to a small minor planet at the mercy of the cosmic weather, he has yet to establish an assuredly commanding place for his ends in this world. In sum, the human being is a complex purposive being still immensely insecure in a vast causal universe. Clearly, to be successful, to reach his best on all fronts, his causal position must be greatly strengthened as his telic diversity must be developed in accordance with its principles to full eminence.

So far as the good life of its members is concerned, a good society, I believe, would be specifically devoted to these two tasks. It would be a society whose aim was an inwardly well-developed people in a mechanically secure world. What would this mean? At a minimum, two things.

First, it would mean that as a matter of social habit or general institutional practice each individual would be treated equally and impartially, on his own merits, as an intrinsically purposive creature, or as an originative center of purposive striving. Only under this condition could his capacities develop the inherent range in whose proper exercise the good life consists. But, second, physical potentials progressively unlocked by the natural sciences would be treated as *humane* resources to aid or assist individuals, not, as they frequently are now, to threaten, delude, harm, and even destroy individuals. Only under this condition would technology and the causal sciences genuinely strengthen the human being's mechanical position, and starting at home, here on earth, begin to wipe out the insecurities of this position that still everywhere beset him. Should a society achieve or try to achieve these two conditions it would be doing at least the minimum of what it could do to have an inwardly well-developed people in mechanically secure circumstances.

Two deviations from such a society are obviously possible. In the first, the individual, being treated as a means, would be expected to fit into some *a priori* social pattern. A harmony of activities might result from a conformity induced by force or habit or persuasion. But exploitation for an end extrinsic to the individual would be the rule, and the telic potential of the individual would be leveled to fit this goal. Unity of purpose might be achieved in the society but at the expense of diversity and richness. In the second type, physical resources might be developed extensively but as instruments of partisan competition. The aim would be the triumph of some individual or group at the expense of other individuals or groups, and the causal power of individuals would be thinned or destroyed as necessary for strengthening the power position of a small segment. Richness on a small or provincial scale might be achieved, but at the risk, and even at the expense, of rending or destroying the larger social fabric. Under either society, it seems plain, the good life as a general phenomenon would be simply impossible. A few might seem to have it, for example those whose goals fell easily and effectively within the loops of subservience or exploitation. Yet even such people might be troubled if they should try to look upon their world as a setting in which a human being could act freely or securely, without compromising his possibilities.

The good society, we say, is one whose aim is an inwardly well-developed people in a world as mechanically secure as possible. Morality in it, indeed the good life itself, would be rooted in material being and culminate in inner excellence. Thus, the good life, the congenial and effective life, and the good society as here conceived, sharing an equal concern for inner individual strength and outer public mastery, would be two halves of the same whole.

To determine what such a society would require in detail and how to establish it, for example, the kind of institutions: law, government, and other agencies, and the kind of attitudes: the roles of imagination, habit, tolerance, would be a major task of the value science investigating the social structure. On its practical side alone, or how to establish it, many people believe that a sufficiently rapid transformation of peoples today into a pacific society of rational creatures, such as a good society would be, is a herculean task far beyond human power. They forecast a new Ice Age for human beings. The interminable large-scale power conflicts, the mediocrity and vulgarity of our social life, the flaccidity toward large ideas, the vast anxieties and fears driving multitudes of people to return in panic to ancient superstition: these seem to testify to a widespread degeneracy and an incompetence to entertain, even less to execute, a rational concept of human betterment. It may be so. But it may be that such a view reflects only temporary sensational aspects of the current situation and has no profound implications for the future. In our present state of social knowledge, descriptions are often incomplete and forecasts very uncertain. Also, where the rewards of a society lie, the mass of talent tends to congregate, and a slight change in one of the variables of a society often alters the total outlook.

In any case, the chief point remains that the good life of the individual in its full range and measure depends on an appropriate social context. He can go only a limited distance toward its complex and demanding ends without environing opportunities in a favorable setting. Meanwhile, like other value principles, the idea of a good society, possible of realization or not, now or in the future, can function as a standard to measure the value of present society and delineate the requirements of the good society of the future. In this respect, like all value principles, it serves the first practical goal—but not the ultimate practical goal—of a value science.

Cosmological

Although we have stated throughout that our analysis was limited to human values, we have occasionally suggested that value may have a larger field, that, even if there were no human beings, other things might have value for each other and in their own right, and indeed, that value might be truly cosmic in range. In the history of Western philosophy this is not an unfamiliar conception, as we have already noted. Spinoza defined value or perfection as the amount of power or potency in a thing, and found a principle of self-assertion or power, *conatus*, in every thing. Similar views can be found throughout Western history from Socrates and Plato to McTaggart and Whitehead.

In terms of our own view, such a conception would mean that every thing or continuant[3] has a *telos* or directional principle. The contour of the career of this thing would be crucially determined by its own nature, just as the path of a particle in physics is said to be determined, so far as it is determined, by the particle's own position and velocity. In physical things this resident directionality

---

[3] D. W. Gotshalk, *Structure and Reality* (New York: Dial Press, 1937), Chaps. I and VI.

is rather simple, and can be quantified, and it does not interest us in itself, nor need it ordinarily, since we are normally interested in physical things only for some purpose of our own. But it is there, clearly, if perhaps oversimply, and expressed in particular physical transactions and by such general concepts as the Second Law of Thermodynamics. This principle of resident directionality in things begins to assume noticeable scope and complexity, however, when we turn to living beings, particularly to the higher animals. Human beings stand at the apex of this telic hierarchy, having the most complex directional resources, including reflective bents that do not seem to be possessed by any other type of finite individual.[4]

Perhaps human beings truly miss the full savor of life when in pursuit of self-centered ends they do not see all things as having similar ends, and enjoy the universe as a value spectacle. But our reason for introducing these observations is not to expound a particular cosmological concept of value on its merits, but to set the stage for considering a speculation that has bearing on our theory of the principle of human value and our view of the good life for human beings.

This speculation contends that all things are value centers, and that the universe is a system of such centers; and in these respects, it agrees with the cosmological view we have just been expounding. But this speculation also holds that the principle of value of these centers is imposed upon them. This idea is subtly suggested by Whitehead when he says that aesthetic values "arise from the culmination, in some sense, of the brooding presence of the whole on to its various parts."[5] It is stated in more explicit but more limited terms by Descartes, who describes the principle of perfection or value as implanted in the finite human creature by God at birth, an image of the Maker stamped on his work.[6] It is given a most detailed statement by Aquinas, who conceives each entity in the universe as a creation of a perfect Being, the whole creation manifesting His perfection, and each component imperfect frag-

---

[4] *Ibid.*, Chap. I. Of all the animals, man alone has a theoretical science and philosophy, or indeed any symbolic structures developed for their reflective values.

[5] Alfred North Whitehead, *Science and the Modern World* (New York: Macmillan Co., 1925), p. 127.

[6] Rene Descartes, *Meditations on First Philosophy*, Meditation III.

ment having a longing for this perfection and, in seeking good, seeking God. Not only is the principle of value of these creatures derived from "outside" but their destination or goal as centers of striving and value is a transcendent life.[7]

However comforting or correct these speculations may be, the point we wish to make is that they have no connection with our own views. We have set forth a telic concept of man, even advocated the primacy of the telic in man. But this has been on empirical grounds, not as a deduction from a supernaturalism. The human being acts from desires, drives, bents, goal-seeking directional impulses. These are fundamental in his everyday behavior and the basic clues to it. He is telic in this crude matter-of-fact sense. Also, according to our account, the principles of human value, as all telic principles, are certified not by their high origin but by their own merits. Any telic principle of the human creature to be a certified principle of value must do the job of such a principle, or meet the requirements of the principle which are imbedded in it.

This position is not only obviously different from the theological view above stated, which locates the basic principle of value outside mundane human experience. It also has three implications of capital importance for human value theory which should be briefly mentioned.

First, since human values and the principle of these values reside in the very structure and substance of human experience, our position implies that human value problems can be attacked and in principle solved definitively by properly understood empirical method. Second, it implies that human value studies in various areas can be conducted with a certain autonomy, having a subject matter of their own and principles that can be assessed by interior means. This is the possibility of value science specialization. Finally, above all, the position implies that the human value sciences can be set up, solidly, independent of a theological base, and can have the kind of freedom similar to that which the natural sciences won several centuries ago and have enjoyed ever since. This third implication, which seems absolutely crucial for any sound proposal of a new set of value sciences, is sufficient in itself, I believe, to make such a position as we have taken of major consequence.

---

[7] St. Thomas Aquinas, *Summa contra Gentiles,* trans. by Joseph Rickaby (London: Burns and Oates, 1905), Vol. II, pp. 45 ff.

Having now sharply separated our views on teleology and on the principle of value from certain traditional theological conceptions, let me state briefly, following an earlier account,[8] a cosmological speculation that seems consistent both with the general immanent teleology described at the opening of this section, and with our theory of human value and the good human life.

If we think of God as Being in its supreme form or the whole of Being, it is evident that to describe God as an originator of anything, value or whatever, is to be guilty of a contradiction. To originate means to produce something new. Finite beings might originate. Indeed, they are the only known source of all that has origins. But as the whole of being there is nothing not already actual in God's being, and so no new actual being that He could originate. However, in each finite human being, there is a will to make a whole of each deed that seems good, and even of a life, and this impetus to wholeness is embodied in all principles of value which by their nature are required to enclose the complete set of distinctive value possibilities in the area they aim to govern. Thus, while human nature has its own immanent ends, these ends reflect a higher order of existence. Wholeness, which man seeks, is already fulfilled in what God is. There is a kind of cosmic confirmation for every valid telic pattern, for every good deed, and for every good life.

If we should be asked "Why should I be good?" the answer of our whole account is: because good is *good* and there is nothing better, except more of good. The good is its own justification for being. But if we were asked for a cosmological outlook most consonant with our concept of the good, we would set aside the traditional theory for one such as just outlined.

Finally, it may not be amiss to indicate the conception of religion that fits into our views. Superstition, fear, loneliness, moral failure, self-seeking, are a few of the numerous motives that lead people to join in organized worship. But religion is not necessarily connected with any of these, nor with the regional mythologies that usually adorn it. In essentials its chief feature is veneration of perfection or of the pattern of the good embodied in the supreme form of Being. Such veneration inevitably leads to corroboration of the good life in its other parts. But it would be a mistake, I believe, to think of religion as chiefly concerned with this afterglow.

---

[8] Gotshalk, *Structure and Reality*, Chap. VIII.

Its primary concern, I think, is with the higher life, the awareness of the form of the good life as enshrined in completeness of being. It is a life that in its fullness the ordinary man usually knows only dimly, in the farthest reaches of consciousness. But a segment of being is given to him at every moment of his existence, and by the power of his brain and the telic impulses of his soul he can foreshadow the whole. Religion springs from this transforming outlook, and transcends ordinary time, change, and circumstance. Its vision is to see the form of the good at a glance in its final embodied perfection from one's tiny window on eternity.

INDEX OF PROPER NAMES